The Central Government-Funded Teacher Education Policy in China

This book utilises expectancy–value theory and undermining effect of extrinsic reward theory to examine the impact of the Central Government-Funded Teacher Education (CGFTE) policy on Chinese pre-service teachers' motivations for choosing the teaching profession.

Quantitative data analysis revealed six distinct categories of motivations to teach: teacher influence, job advantages (extrinsic), social value (altruistic), personal interest (intrinsic), others' suggestions, and fallback career. These categories were further exemplified in ten narrative stories. The findings indicate that the CGFTE policy attracts high-school graduates with higher intrinsic motivation to enrol in teacher-training programs, but it seems ineffective in increasing their intrinsic career-choice motivation. It is argued that the CGFTE policy, which emphasises extrinsic benefits but limits professional development, does not have a significant negative impact on pre-service teachers' motivation to choose teaching. This conclusion is supported by the offsetting effects of the policy's restrictive and encouraging aspects, as explained by expectancy–value theory and the qualitative data. Nevertheless, the intrinsic motivation of policy-funded pre-service teachers did not improve as much as that of their self-supported counterparts, indicating potential undermining effects of the policy. The study concludes by discussing the implications of these findings for enhancing the CGFTE policy, teacher training, and career education in China.

The book will be an essential read for students and scholars of higher education, Chinese studies, and educational studies in general.

Dr. Yi Liu is a faculty member at Southwest University in China, specialising in teaching pedagogy to pre-service teachers and international students. He holds a PhD in Education from the University of Canterbury in New Zealand. Dr. Liu's research focuses on teacher education and the enhancement of educational policies.

China Perspectives

The *China Perspectives* series focuses on translating and publishing works by leading Chinese scholars, writing about both global topics and China-related themes. It covers humanities & social sciences, education, media and psychology, as well as many interdisciplinary themes.

This is the first time any of these books have been published in English for international readers. The series aims to put forward a Chinese perspective, give insights into cutting-edge academic thinking in China, and inspire researchers globally.

To submit proposals, please contact the Taylor & Francis Publisher for China Publishing Programme, Lian Sun (Lian.Sun@informa.com)

Titles in education currently include:

Migration and Educational Policymaking in China
A Critical Engagement with Policy Sociology and Bourdieu
Hui Yu

Reimaging Pre-Service Teachers' Practical Knowledge
Designing Learning for Future
Ge Wei

Precise Poverty Alleviation and Intergenerational Mobility in China
Chunking Chen

Interaction and Knowledge Construction in Online English Teaching
A Learning Analytics Perspective
Yining Zhang

The Central Government-Funded Teacher Education Policy in China
Impacts on Career-Choice Motivation of Pre-service Teachers
Yi Liu

For more information, please visit www.routledge.com/China-Perspectives/book-series/CPH

The Central Government-Funded Teacher Education Policy in China
Impacts on Career-Choice Motivation of Pre-service Teachers

Yi Liu

LONDON AND NEW YORK

This work was supported by the Humanities and Social Sciences Youth Foundation, Ministry of Education of the People's Republic of China (Grant No. 19XJC880004); the Fundamental Research Funds for the Central Universities (Grant No. SWU1809721); and the China Scholarship Council (Grant No. 2011699013).

First published 2024
by Routledge
4 Park Square, Milton Park, Abingdon, Oxon OX14 4RN

and by Routledge
605 Third Avenue, New York, NY 10158

Routledge is an imprint of the Taylor & Francis Group, an informa business

© 2024 Yi Liu

The right of Yi Liu to be identified as author of this work has been asserted in accordance with sections 77 and 78 of the Copyright, Designs and Patents Act 1988.

All rights reserved. No part of this book may be reprinted or reproduced or utilised in any form or by any electronic, mechanical, or other means, now known or hereafter invented, including photocopying and recording, or in any information storage or retrieval system, without permission in writing from the publishers.

Trademark notice: Product or corporate names may be trademarks or registered trademarks, and are used only for identification and explanation without intent to infringe.

British Library Cataloguing-in-Publication Data
A catalogue record for this book is available from the British Library

Library of Congress Cataloging-in-Publication Data
Names: Liu, Yi, 1984- author.
Title: The central government-funded teacher education policy in China : impacts on career-choice motivation of pre-service teachers / Yi Liu.
Description: First edition. | New York : Routledge, 2024. | Series: China perspectives | Includes bibliographical references and index.
Identifiers: LCCN 2023033548 (print) | LCCN 2023033549 (ebook) | ISBN 9781032639673 (hbk) | ISBN 9781032639703 (pbk) | ISBN 9781032639680 (ebk)
Subjects: LCSH: Student teachers—Training of—China. | Student teachers—China—Attitudes. | Motivation in education—China. | Teaching—Vocational guidance—China. | Education and state—China.
Classification: LCC LB2157.C6 L58 2024 (print) | LCC LB2157.C6 (ebook) | DDC 370.71/10951—dc23/eng/20230913
LC record available at https://lccn.loc.gov/2023033548
LC ebook record available at https://lccn.loc.gov/2023033549

ISBN: 978-1-032-63967-3 (hbk)
ISBN: 978-1-032-63970-3 (pbk)
ISBN: 978-1-032-63968-0 (ebk)

DOI: 10.4324/9781032639680

Typeset in Times New Roman
by Apex CoVantage, LLC

Contents

	List of Figures	*vi*
	List of Tables	*vii*
	Acknowledgements	*viii*
	List of Abbreviations	*ix*
1	Background and Rationale for Conducting This Study	1
2	Literature Review	17
3	Mixed-Methods Research Design	40
4	Quantitative Analysis of Data From 712 Chinese Pre-service Teachers and Results	47
5	Narrative Stories of Ten Policy-Funded Pre-Service Teachers and Reflections	66
6	Discussion, Recommendations, Limitations, and Conclusions	87
	Appendices	*99*
	Index	*108*

Figures

4.1	Province Distribution of the 712 Participants' Homes	50
4.2	Scree Test for Component Analysis on the CCM Scale Reduced to 29 Variables	55
4.3	Graphical Display of Interaction Effects of Personal Interest (Intrinsic Motivation) Across Groups of Funding Status by Gender	61
4.4	Graphical Display of Interaction Effects of Personal Interest (Intrinsic Motivation) Across Groups of Funding Status by Year of Study	62

Tables

1.1	Classification of Key Terms of the CGFTE Policy	7
4.1	Extraction of Component Factors for the CCM Scale Reduced to 29 Variables	54
4.2	Oblique-Rotated Component Analysis Pattern Matrix of the CCM Scale Reduced to 29 Variables	56
4.3	Career-Choice Motivations and Their Importance Ranking among Chinese Pre-service Teachers (N = 712)	57
4.4	Independent-Samples T-Test Results for the Career-Choice Motivations of PFPTs vs. SSPTs	59
4.5	Between-Subjects Effects for Group Differences in Personal Interest Across Groups of Funding Status by Gender	60
4.6	Between-Subjects Effects for Group Differences in Personal Interest Across Groups of Funding Status by Year of Study	61
5.1	Demographic Information of the Ten Interviewees	67

Acknowledgements

This book is based on my PhD thesis, which was completed in 2016 at the University of Canterbury, New Zealand. I would like to express my sincere gratitude to Professor John Everatt and Professor Janinka Greenwood for their unwavering support and expertise. Their guidance and feedback played a pivotal role in shaping the content of this work. I am also thankful to Professor Helen Watt and Professor Paul Richardson for granting permission to use their scale in this book and to Professor Emily Lin for providing the original Chinese translation of the scale.

I am deeply grateful to my beloved wife, Lina Peng, for her support throughout the revising process. Her meticulous proofreading and invaluable suggestions have greatly enhanced the quality of this book. I am also immensely thankful to my newborn daughter, Hanyue Liu, for being a constant source of encouragement throughout the writing process. Heartfelt thanks go to my parents for their loving care and assistance in looking after my daughter, allowing me to dedicate my full attention to completing this book.

Dr. Yi Liu
Faculty of Education,
Southwest University, Chongqing, China

Abbreviations

ANOVA	Analysis of Variance
CCM scale	Career-Choice Motivation Scale
EM Approach	Expectation Maximisation Approach
EVT	Expectancy-Value Theory
FIT-Choice scale	Factors Influencing Teaching Choice Scale
CGFTE policy	Central Government-Funded Teacher Education Policy
IMF	International Monetary Fund
MSA	Measure of Sample Adequacy
NCEE	National College Entrance Examination
PCA	Principal Component Analysis
PFPTs	Policy-Funded Pre-service Teachers
SPSS	Statistic Package for Social Science
SSPTs	Self-Sponsored Pre-service Teachers
UEER theory	Undermining Effect of Extrinsic Reward Theory

1 Background and Rationale for Conducting This Study

Introduction

Modern teacher education in China has experienced changes between whether to charge pre-service teachers for tuition and other fees or not. Since 2007, the Chinese central government has implemented the Central Government-Funded Teacher Education (CGFTE) policy, which makes teacher education free again in the six key national teacher training universities. The CGFTE policy addresses the need to provide quality teachers for schools in China and ensure continuous teaching service. Accordingly, the policy provides select students with free tuition and an allowance for living costs and binds them to a period of teaching service after graduation, some of which will be in rural schools.

Since the start of this funding policy, however, contradictory views have been raised about how it shapes Chinese pre-service teachers' motivation to choose teaching as a profession. These views are echoed in expectancy–value theory (EVT) and in the undermining effect of extrinsic reward theory, which suggest that CGFTE policy provisions could have influences on the career-choice motivation of pre-service teachers. To explore the specific impacts of this funding policy on Chinese pre-service teachers' career-choice motivation, this study applies a mixed-methods approach and designs two quantitative and one qualitative sub-questions to unpack the research purpose.

1.1 Brief History of Modern, Tuition-Free Teacher Education in China

In the history of modern teacher education in China, pre-service teachers have been granted various preferential benefits including exemption from tuition fees. However, there have been short periods of time when pre-service teachers were required to pay fees. Throughout their history, teacher education policies in China have undergone a series of "pendulum" changes regarding the issue of whether or not to charge pre-service teachers tuition fees (Sun, 2018).

DOI: 10.4324/9781032639680-1

2 *Background and Rationale for Conducting This Study*

During the late Qing Dynasty, the first modern teacher-training colleges in China were established, including the Nanyang Public School Teacher Education Institute (Nanyang gongxue shifangyuan) in 1896 and the Imperial University Teacher College (Jingshi daxuetang shifanguan) in 1902. These institutions were fully funded by the government, covering all costs for pre-service teachers. Graduates were then required to teach for a designated period of time (Qu & Yuan, 2010). In 1912, the provisional government of the Republic of China promulgated the Teacher Education Act (Shifan jiaoyu ling) and the Teacher-Training School Regulation (Shifan xuexiao guicheng), which stipulated that some pre-service teachers in teacher-training schools would be fully or partially funded while others were self-funded (Cui, 2006).

From 1922 onward, with the implementation of the New Education System (Renxu xuezhi), teacher-training schools in various provinces merged with local high schools. This allowed for integrating teacher education with agriculture, industry, and business education programs, which had traditionally been self-funded (Wang, 1985). As a result, some high schools gradually eliminated government-funded teacher education, and bills were proposed to cancel it, such as in the province of Zhejiang (Cui, 2006). However, self-sponsored teacher education was not approved by the Nanjing Nationalist Government founded in 1927, and teacher education in China gradually became free again. The Law for Teacher-Training Schools (Shifan xuexiao fa), enacted in 1932, formulated that teacher-training schools, special education programs, and pre-school education programs should not charge tuition fees to students (Qu & Yuan, 2010). Similar statements can be found in other government regulations, such as the Teacher-Training School Regulations (Shifan xuexiao guicheng) in 1938 and the Approaches to Implement Government-Funded Education for Students in National Teacher-Training Schools (Quanguo shifan xuexiao xuesheng gongfei daiyu shishi banfa) in 1944 issued by the Nationalist Government.

After the founding of the People's Republic of China in 1949, university students were exempted from paying tuition fees, and pre-service teachers were eligible for monthly subsidies to cover living costs under the People's Subsidies Scheme (Renmin zhuxuejing zhidu). This lasted for several decades until official documents were released between 1985 and 1996 that constantly modified the People's Subsidies Scheme (Mei, 2008). Although most pre-service teachers in teacher-training universities still enjoyed many preferential policies, including scholarship and subsidy schemes, in contrast with other university students, these modifications signalled that reforms in teacher education were on the horizon (Zhang, 2007).

The year 1997 marked a turning point in teacher education in China, as both the quantity and quality of pre-service teachers declined following the implementation of gradual charging systems in teacher-training colleges and universities (Mei, 2008). An official document (State Council, 1994, p. 723) proposed that college students should pay their own fees and be free to find

Background and Rationale for Conducting This Study 3

their own jobs. It was scheduled that most higher education institutions would meet this requirement by 1997 and that by 2000, the transformation from old education systems to new ones would be completed. Starting from 2003, all pre-service teachers were charged fees at teacher education institutions, symbolising the end of free teacher education in China.

From around 2000 to 2007, higher education reforms in China required pre-service teachers to pay their own fees, and some teacher-training universities were gradually transformed into comprehensive institutions. These reforms were intended to increase financial resources for teacher-training universities and enhance the professional levels of teacher education, but they had negative effects. In response to these problems, a new teacher education policy was issued in 2007 that made teacher education free again in the top-level teacher-training universities in China.

1.2 Introduction of the Central Government-Funded Teacher Education Policy

1.2.1 Contexts for Implementing the Policy

Prior to the implementation of the Central Government-Funded Teacher Education (CGFTE) policy, China encountered several challenges with teacher education and the distribution of quality teachers from 1997 to 2007. Firstly, the characteristics of teacher education weakened and shifted owing to fierce competition and challenges during the ongoing and in-depth reform of the higher education system (Mei, 2008). Many teacher-training institutions transformed into comprehensive universities, resulting in fewer education programs and fewer pre-service teachers. Consequently, the distinctive characteristics of teacher training gradually dissipated.

During this time, the quality of pre-service teachers also appeared to decline (Li, 2007). Self-funded teacher education negatively impacted the motivations of talented high school graduates from disadvantaged backgrounds to pursue teacher-training programs, and the increased number of tertiary education opportunities beginning in 1999 provided more options for high school graduates to select non-education programs at universities. These factors led to the decline in the quality of pre-service teachers, which reflected the weakened appeal of teacher-training programs and the teaching profession to outstanding high school graduates.

Pre-service teachers were particularly less likely to pursue a career in teaching in rural-area schools (Liu et al., 2002). Between 1997 and 2007, many graduates from teacher-education programs in China ended up in jobs other than teaching, pursuing master's degrees or studying abroad. According to a comprehensive survey conducted by Liu et al. (2002), about 25% pre-service teachers in 2002 did not enter teaching positions after graduation. Additionally, those who chose to teach tended to prefer teaching in key public

4 Background and Rationale for Conducting This Study

or private schools with higher salaries, with only a few willing to teach in ordinary or "weak" schools (Liu et al., 2002). These factors contributed to an already imbalanced distribution of quality teachers in China, with too few teaching staff in rural-area schools located in the west or inland China and an excess in urban-area schools (Liu et al., 2002).

Lastly, the gap between poor rural-area schools and developed urban-area schools was conspicuous, with rural schools commonly lacking educational resources and facilities and attended by students from lower socioeconomic backgrounds who struggled to gain parental support (Liu, 2010). These inferior aspects put rural education at a disadvantage, making it difficult to attract and maintain a teaching force in rural-area schools in China (Chen, 2003; Lin, 2010). The large population of unqualified teachers in poor rural-area schools in turn posed a significant challenge to the quality and equality of compulsory education in the country as a whole (Paine & Fang, 2009).

One of the measures proposed to solve these problems was the CGFTE policy, introduced by the Ministry of Education of China in January 2007 in the Key Working Points of Year 2007 (Erlinglingqi nian gongzuo yaodian). Two months later, former Premier of China Wen Jiabao presented the policy in the Government Work Report (Zhengfu gongzuo baogao). On 9 May 2007, the State Council released the official document of the CGFTE Policy (Trial) in Teacher-Training Universities Directly under the Ministry of Education of China (Jiaoyubu zhishu shifandaxue shifansheng mianfei jiaoyu shishi banfa <shixing>), marking the return of free teacher education in national key teacher-training universities in China. Five years later, a supplementary document, Opinions on Improving and Promoting the CGFTE (Guanyu wanshan he tuijin shifansheng mianfei jiaoyu de yijian), was promulgated. On 30 July 2018, an updated and formal version of the CGFTE policy was subsequently enacted by the State Council (General Office of the State Council of China, 2018).

1.2.2 Goals of the Policy

The purposes of the CGFTE policy, according to the Central Government Annual Report in 2007 (Wen, 2007), were to create a social atmosphere where teachers and the teaching profession were highly respected, to develop a large number of high-quality teachers, and to encourage young people to devote themselves to lifelong teaching. Similarly, the sixth press conference of the Ministry of Education in 2007 (Song, 2007) concluded that the intentions of the policy were (1) to encourage excellent high school graduates with teaching ambitions to choose teacher-training programs; (2) to support pre-service teachers in teaching for a long time and in rural schools; (3) to promote teacher education reforms of enrolment and pedagogy; and (4) to clarify education orientations and goals for the six policy universities.

Some researchers believe that implementing the CGFTE policy was also significant for improving educational equality and teacher quality in China. It provided excellent students from poor families with a chance to attend higher education and hence become high-quality teachers, and it helped to ease the ever-increasing problem of the uneven distribution of high-quality teachers across dissimilar communities (e.g., Liu, 2010; Mei, 2008).

1.2.3 Contents of the Policy

According to the official documents published by the General Office of the State Council of China (2007, 2018), the main contents of the CGFTE policy were as follows:

(i) The CGFTE policy has been implemented since September 2007 in the six national key teacher-training universities that are subordinated to the Ministry of Education. These universities include Beijing Normal University, East China Normal University, Northeast Normal University, Central China Normal University, Shaanxi Normal University, and Southwest University.
(ii) The teacher-education programs of the six universities that carry out the policy have the priority of recruiting excellent high-school graduates who are interested in teaching and commit to teaching long term.
(iii) Under this policy, the pre-service teachers (known as policy-funded pre-service teachers, PFPTs) are exempt from all tuition and accommodation fees and receive an allowance to cover their living costs. All these expenses are paid by the Central Government.
(iv) Before enrolling in any of the six policy universities, the PFPTs are required to sign a contract with both the university and the Provincial Executive Department of Education promising to teach in a primary or secondary school for at least six years after graduation. Additionally, they must teach in a rural-area school for one year if they work in a city school.[1] The Chinese government encourages PFPT graduates to teach for a lifetime. Those who violate the contract after graduation are subject to repayment of all the fees originally waived during their university studies, as well as fines.[2] The Provincial Executive Department of Education is responsible for managing the contract and creating a credit record for the PFPTs. In exceptional cases, the PFPTs may receive permission from the Provincial Executive Department of Education to cancel their contracts.
(v) After attending a policy university, the PFPTs have the chance to change to another major among the university's available teacher-training programs. During the first year of university study, they can even switch to a non-education program if they are determined to be unsuitable for teaching and reimburse the tuition and fees. Meanwhile, undergraduates majoring in other programs at the same university can switch to government-funded teacher-education programs within their first two years of study if they commit to becoming teachers after graduation. Those who successfully transfer will receive retrospective funding for their previous payments and will be treated the same as other PFPTs thereafter.

(vi) PFPT graduates are generally required to return to and teach in their home provinces. The local provincial government ensures that every PFPT graduate who adheres to the contract can obtain an official teaching post at a primary or secondary school. Additionally, the Provincial Executive Department of Education takes responsibility for arranging job fairs for schools to recruit new staff and for PFPT graduates to choose a school to teach in. During their periods of teaching service, the PFPT graduates can transfer among schools and even perform educational management jobs.

(vii) Generally, PFPTs are not permitted to take examinations to become academic postgraduates during the period of their undergraduate studies and teaching services. However, as compensation, PFPT graduates who meet certain national standards can enrol as professional postgraduates in education without taking the exams, and they can complete courses through remote learning while they teach. If they pass the thesis exam and their teaching service is satisfactory, they will be awarded a postgraduate diploma and a professional master's degree.

(viii) The six teacher-training universities should view the CGFTE policy as an opportunity to promote teacher education reform for cultivating high-quality teachers and educators. They need to design their teacher-training programs carefully, according to the needs of basic education development and reforms. This includes appointing famous teacher educators as tutors, reinforcing moral education, and establishing a sound system for PFPT teaching internships for at least one semester. The PFPTs are expected to have modern educational concepts, a passion for teaching careers, and a willingness to teach for an extended period so they can become excellent teachers or even educational experts.

(ix) The quality of primary and secondary school teachers who graduate from the six teacher-training universities should be set as their educational quality indicator. Universities that make significant contributions to educating pre-service teachers will be more favourably supported by the central government in terms of funding.

(x) Provincial governments, educational departments, and universities that share responsibilities to carry out the CGFTE policy should be aware of its importance and profound influence. They should take responsibility and work together to ensure the successful implementation of this policy. Local governments should take effective measures to encourage and support PFPT graduates who do teach long term. Funding from the central government will tend to support schools in the middle and western areas of China where PFPT graduate. Local governments and rural-area schools should guarantee basic living conditions and temporary housing for PFPT graduates who teach and serve there.

Background and Rationale for Conducting This Study 7

According to their contents and requirements, the policy terms above can be categorised into two types (refer to Table 1.1): encouraging or restrictive. Encouraging terms focus on how to attract excellent high school graduates to choose the teacher education majors in universities and become primary and secondary school teachers; restrictive terms mainly address how to ensure that students who receive government-sponsored teacher education complete their studies and fulfil their long-term teaching commitments in primary and secondary schools.

Table 1.1 Classification of Key Terms of the CGFTE Policy

Classification	No.	Contents
Encouraging Terms	1	The policy-funded pre-service teachers (PFPTs) receive a waiver of tuition and accommodation fees, as well as a cost-of-living subsidy, during their four-year undergraduate studies.
	2	The teacher-training programs of the six key national universities provide advanced enrolment to qualified high school graduates.
	3	The PFPTs have a chance to change their original major at university.
	4	Local governments involved are required to take actions to ensure that every PFPT graduate who obeys the contract can obtain a teaching job in a primary or secondary school.
	5	PFPT graduates can transfer among different schools or take on roles in school management during their teaching services.
	6	PFPT graduates who meet the necessary requirements are eligible to enrol and become non-academic postgraduates without attending examinations.
	7	Local governments and schools in rural areas are obligated to provide basic living conditions, including temporary accommodation, for PFPT graduates teaching in these areas.
Restrictive Terms	8	All top six national teacher-training universities implement the CGFTE policy and exclusively recruit PFPTs.
	9	Before enrolling in one of these universities, each PFPT must sign an agreement with the university and the government committing to teaching for at least six years.
	10	After graduation, PFPTs must teach and serve in rural-area schools for at least one year if they plan to work in a city school.
	11	Graduates of PFPTs who breach the agreement without valid reasons must repay all fees and are subject to fines according to the agreement.
	12	The Educational Executive Department of the Province is responsible for handling breaches of contract and maintaining a credit archive for each PFPT.
	13	PFPT graduates usually teach in primary or secondary schools located in their home provinces.
	14	Before and after graduation, PFPTs are not permitted to take examinations to become academic postgraduates.

8 Background and Rationale for Conducting This Study

1.3 Contradictory Views on the Career-Choice Motivations of Pre-service Teachers Funded by the CGFTE Policy

Ever since the launch of the CGFTE policy in 2007, thousands of students each year have enrolled in the teacher-training programs funded by the policy. These students bring their own personal experiences, expectations, values, and perceptions to their chosen teacher-training universities. Each of them has a reason for enrolling in a specific teacher-education program, and their level of engagement in that program largely reflects the responsibilities associated with their choice (Pittaway, 2012). Although the CGFTE policy was perceived as a "new and innovative teacher education policy with Chinese characteristics" (Li et al., 2013, p. 44), there are still many public concerns about the policy (Gao & Chang, 2014; Jiang, 2014; Shen & Cai, 2019). Among them, the question about whether the CGFTE policy impacts the career-choice motivation of pre-service teachers has captured the attention of researchers.

Different views regarding this question can be found in various studies. Some believe that students who choose to enter the teacher-education programs funded by the policy are motivated by extrinsic benefits rather than by a genuine interest in becoming a teacher (Wang & Niu, 2023; Wu & Liu, 2008; Zhou, 2013). These arguments are based on the various benefits provided by the CGFTE policy, including exemption from tuition and accommodation fees and a regular allowance to cover living costs during students' four-year undergraduate studies. After graduation, employment is guaranteed, and the option of professional postgraduate study is available. These studies suggest that these benefits attract individuals who are mainly interested in the extrinsic rewards provided by the CGFTE policy and who consequently do not study hard in these programs. As a result, the teaching quality of teachers who graduate from the teacher-training programs funded by the policy may be lower than that of other teachers, and more attention should be paid to the negative incentives of the CGFTE policy (Di et al., 2022).

Other researchers, however, hold a different opinion on this issue. Their studies show that those who have a strong interest in teaching are more likely to choose government-funded teacher-training programs (Wang, 2011). As stated in the provisions of the CGFTE policy, graduates of the policy-funded programs are required to provide teaching services for a minimum of six years, including one year of teaching in a rural-area school. Breaching this educational service contract will result in a refund of all higher education payments and heavy fines. These restrictive terms could limit the choice of government-funded teacher-training programs to those who have a strong personal interest in teaching long term because "if they break their promise, it will be very costly for them" (Li et al., 2013, p. 57). Moreover, to successfully complete the six-year teaching services, those students with high intrinsic motivation to teach will work hard to master teaching skills during their teacher education.

These seemingly contradictory views on the career-choice motivation of pre-service teachers funded by the CGFTE policy require further exploration through scientific research designs. Existing literature has tied pre-service teachers' motivation to teach to teacher education outcomes (König & Rothland, 2012), commitment to the teaching profession (e.g., Serow, 1994; Wang & Fwu, 2001), engagement in the teaching profession (e.g., Fokkens-Bruinsma & Canrinus, 2014; Wong et al., 2014), and teacher retention (e.g., Ding & Sun, 2007; Lin et al., 2012; Richardson & Watt, 2010). Results from exploring the career-choice motivations of policy-funded pre-service teachers could provide important information for policy-makers and teacher educators to assess whether the CGFTE policy is proceeding on the right track towards its initial target of developing a stable teaching force, especially for poor rural areas.

1.4 Definition of Key Terms

Two key terms in this study currently lack commonly accepted definitions in the literature. To avoid any confusion, this study provides operational definitions for them:

(i) Policy-funded pre-service teachers (PFPTs) are teacher candidates in China who are attending teacher-training programs at the six universities that are currently implementing the CGFTE policy. They differ from other teacher candidates in two significant ways. Firstly, their four-year teacher education is fully funded by the central government, and secondly, they have a clear career path that requires them to return to their home provinces to teach for at least six years, including one year in a rural school.

(ii) The career-choice motivation of PFPTs refers to why they chose teaching as their career path. In existing literature, motivations for choosing teaching include teaching advantages (e.g., lengthy holidays, reliable income, job security, and a steady career path), personal interest in teaching (e.g., a longstanding desire to teach and enjoyment of working with children), social value of teaching (e.g., building children's characters, reducing social inequalities, and contributing to social development), positive influence from school teachers, suggestions from significant others, and difficulties in choosing other careers.

1.5 Theoretical Foundations

Various theories explain motivation from different perspectives according to a comprehensive literature review by Graham and Weiner (2012). This study draws on expectancy–value theory (EVT) model and on the undermining effect of extrinsic reward (UEER) theory. The rationale for applying these theories in the current study is introduced below.

1.5.1 Expectancy–Value Theory

EVT has been widely applied in research work on psychology, particularly related to achievement motivation. Based on earlier works, modern EVT defines the expectancy and value constructs in richer ways by connecting them with wider social, cultural, and contextual factors and examining them in real-world situations instead of in the laboratory (Wigfield & Cambria, 2010). Among them, the EVT model developed by Eccles and her colleagues appears to be related to research questions proposed in the present study.

The EVT model (e.g., Eccles, 1987, 2009; Eccles & Wigfield, 1995; Meece et al., 1990; Wigfield, 1994; Wigfield & Cambria, 2010; Wigfield & Eccles, 2000) proposes that educational, vocational, and other achievement-related choices are directly impacted by one's abilities, beliefs, and expectancies for success on the one hand and by the value one attaches to the task on the other (Richardson & Watt, 2014). It is further hypothesised that "expectancy" and "value" are the most immediate or direct predictors of individuals' performance and choices among various educational, professional, and other achievement-related tasks, and the two constructs themselves are influenced by various social, psychological, cultural, and contextual factors.

The definitions of the two key constructs are clearly described in this model. "Expectations for success" refers to individuals' beliefs about how well they can perform on an upcoming task, currently or in the future. It is conceptually distinguished from individuals' beliefs about competence and ability, which assess one's current ability, particularly when compared with that of others. The other construct, value, has both broad and task-specific definitions. The task-specific value in the model that is adopted in the current study refers to the qualities of different tasks and how those qualities influence the individual's desire to perform the task. Values are subjective because they are individuals' own beliefs about an activity. There are four basic achievement task values (Eccles, 2005; Eccles et al., 1983; Wigfield & Eccles, 1992). "Intrinsic value (interest)" refers to the pleasure one gains from completing a specific task; "utility value" refers to the usefulness of the task for an individual's future development; "attainment value (importance)" means the significance one perceives of successfully completing the task, and "cost" is defined as what the individual must give up to perform a task and the anticipated effort required to complete it.

The relationships among these constructs and components is explained in the EVT model of performance and choice developed by Eccles and her colleagues (e.g., Eccles, 1987, 2009; Eccles & Wigfield, 1995; Meece et al., 1990; Wigfield & Eccles, 2000) and comprehensively reviewed by Wigfield and Cambria (2010). The model demonstrates four layers of factors that impact individuals' choices and performance. Specifically, the model proposes that individuals' expectancies for success and subjective task value directly impact their achievement-related choices and performance. In turn, their expectancy and value are influenced by their perceptions of task difficulty, personal ability, personal goals, self-schemata, and affective memories of past events. These beliefs, goals, and memories are affected by factors in the third layer, that is, individuals' perceptions of others' attitudes and expectations for them and their interpretations of the outcomes of previous actions. Both individuals' perceptions and interpretations are influenced by a series of social, cultural, and contextual factors that exist in their society, such as socialisers' beliefs and behaviours, children's achievement-related experiences and aptitudes, and the deep-rooted cultural milieu.

The present study applies the EVT model as one of the theoretical foundations for understanding the impacts of the CGFTE policy on Chinese pre-service teachers' career-choice motivation for two reasons. Firstly, motivation is defined as a process that initiates and sustains goal-oriented activity (Schunk et al., 2007), and according to this definition, motivation can predict whether a person will start an action and persist in it and to what degree that person will engage in it (Wong et al., 2014). Therefore, pre-service teachers' motivation to choose teaching as a profession relates to their achievement-related choices and performance.

Secondly, the opposing encouraging and restrictive roles in the CGFTE policy can influence pre-service teachers' expectancies for success and task-specific value differently. Most of the policy terms that encourage students to choose the policy-funded teacher-education programs, such as "PFPTs are fully funded during their four-year teacher training" and "PFPT graduates are guaranteed employment", could add task-specific values that encourage individuals to become teachers. However, pre-service teachers' expectations for success could be dampened by the restrictive policy terms: "PFPT graduates must teach in rural areas for at least one year" and "PFPTs are not allowed to become an academic postgraduate". According to the EVT, both individuals' expectations for success and task-specific value can directly impact their achievement-related choices and performance. Therefore, it is theoretically likely that the CGFTE policy impacts pre-service teachers' career-choice motivation.

1.5.2 Undermining Effect of Extrinsic Reward Theory

The theory of UEER, also referred to as the "over-justification effect" in some studies (e.g., Akin-Little & Little, 2004; Bright & Penrod, 2009; Lepper et al., 1973; Peters & Vollmer, 2014; Roane et al., 2003; Tang & Hall, 1995), states that individuals lose their intrinsic motivation to perform a task when they are offered an extrinsic reward for performing that same task (Graham & Weiner, 2012). Many researchers (e.g., Cameron et al., 2005; Deci et al., 1999a, 1999b; Hagger & Chatzisarantis, 2011; Murayama et al., 2010; Wiechman & Gurland, 2009) have explored the UEER and tested different boundary conditions of the theory. After reviewing the existing literature, Graham and Weiner (2012) concluded that the undermining effect on intrinsic motivation is most notable when the rewards are tangible rather than symbolic, expected rather than unexpected, and non-contingent rather than contingent on performance as well as for tasks with initially high interest (p. 377).

The encouraging terms of the CGFTE policy seem to meet these conditions. According to the policy terms, high school graduates who choose and are accepted into one of the government-funded teacher-training programs can receive various benefits, including no-fee university education, guaranteed employment, professional postgraduate study opportunity, and availability of school management jobs. All these benefits can be seen as extrinsic rewards because they go beyond the gains from the teaching profession itself and because they are tangible, mainly related to money, job opportunities, and further study opportunities, instead of symbolic. These extrinsic rewards, as stated in the official CGFTE document (General Office of the State Council of China, 2018), are expected by candidates who want to enrol in these teaching programs. Once they are officially accepted into these programs, they start receiving these rewards. Lastly, it is assumed that high school graduates who choose teaching programs have initial interest in the teaching profession, but under UEER theory, the so-called encouraging terms in the CGFTE policy might actually have an undermining effect on Chinese pre-service teachers' intrinsic motivation to choose the teaching profession.

1.6 Overarching Research Question and Sub-questions

The purpose of this study is to investigate the effects of the CGFTE policy on the career-choice motivation of Chinese pre-service teachers and to provide recommendations for enhancing the policy. Towards this aim, the primary research question is:

> Does the CGFTE policy impact the career-choice motivations of Chinese pre-service teachers, and if so, how?

1.6.1 Quantitative Research Questions

To address the overarching research question, two quantitative sub-questions have been formulated:

(i) What are the different career-choice motivations among Chinese pre-service teachers and how important is each type to them?
(ii) How do policy-funded pre-service teachers (PFPTs) compare with self-sponsored pre-service teachers (SSPTs) in terms of career-choice motivation?

In this study, Chinese pre-service teachers are categorised into two groups: those who are fully funded by the CGFTE policy (PFPTs) and those who are self-sponsored (SSPTs). The first sub-question focuses on the career-choice motivation of all Chinese pre-service teachers. The findings about the types of career-choice motivation and their importance will serve as the foundation for analysing quantitative data for the second sub-question. By comparing the PFPTs and the SSPTs in terms of career-choice motivation, the study will provide empirical evidence of the real impacts of the CGFTE policy on Chinese pre-service teachers' motivations to choose teaching.

1.6.2 Qualitative Research Question

Building upon the quantitative research, a qualitative sub-question has been formulated:

> How do PFPTs with different attitudes towards the CGFTE policy explain their motivations for choosing teaching as their future career?

The responses of PFPTs to this qualitative sub-question are expected to provide insightful and comprehensive explanations for their decisions to pursue teaching as a career. These findings will inform further discussions on ways to enhance the CGFTE policy.

Notes

1 From 2007 to 2017, the CGFTE policy required the PFPTs to teach for at least ten years, and two years of their teaching had to be in rural schools. In 2018, the updated CGFTE policy shortened their teaching-service period to six years with one year of rural teaching.
2 According to the contract, the fines are equivalent to 50% of the total fees originally paid by the central government for the PFPTs.

References

Akin-Little, K. A., & Little, S. G. (2004). Re-examining the overjustification effect. *Journal of Behavioral Education*, *13*(3), 179–192.

Bright, C. N., & Penrod, B. (2009). An evaluation of the overjustification effect across multiple contingency arrangements. *Behavioral Interventions*, *24*(3), 185–194.

Cameron, J., Pierce, W. D., Banko, K. M., & Gear, A. (2005). Achievement-based rewards and intrinsic motivation: A test of cognitive mediators. *Journal of Educational Psychology*, *97*(4), 641–655.

Chen, J.-P. (2003). Improve the quality of education in the rural area. *Exploring Education Development*, *23*(11), 14–18.

Cui, Y.-W. (2006). *Zhongguo shifan jiaoyu shi [History of teacher education in China]*. Shan Xi Jiao Yu Chu Ban She.

Deci, E. L., Koestner, R., & Ryan, R. M. (1999a). A meta-analytic review of experiments examining the effects of extrinsic rewards on intrinsic motivation. *Psychological Bulletin*, *125*(6), 627–668.

Deci, E. L., Koestner, R., & Ryan, R. M. (1999b). The undermining effect is a reality after all-extrinsic rewards, task interest, and self-determination: Reply to Eisenberger, Pierce, and Cameron (1999) and Lepper, Henderlong, and Gingras (1999). *Psychological Bulletin*, *125*(6), 692–700.

Di, Y., Feng, S., & Tan, Y. (2022). Jiyu jiaoxue zhiliang de gongfei shifan jiaoyu zhengce yanjiu [Research on the policy-funded normal students' education from the perspective of teaching quality]. *Jiao Yu Ke Xue*, *38*(1), 49–56.

Ding, G., & Sun, M. L. (2007). The qualifications of the teaching force in China. In R. M. Ingersoll (Ed.), *A comparative study of teacher preparation and qualifications in six nations*. Consortium for Policy Research in Education. University of Pennsylvania.

14 Background and Rationale for Conducting This Study

Eccles, J. S. (1987). Gender roles and women's achievement-related decisions. *Psychology of Women Quarterly, 11*(2), 135–171.

Eccles, J. S. (2005). Subjective task value and the Eccles et al. model of achievement-related choice. In A. J. Elliot & C. S. Dweck (Eds.), *Handbook of competence and motivation*. Guilford.

Eccles, J. S. (2009). Who am I and what am I going to do with my life? Personal and collective identities as motivators of action. *Educational Psychologist, 44*(2), 78–89.

Eccles, J. S., Adler, T. F., Futterman, R., Goff, S. B., Kaczala, C. M., & Meece, J. L. (1983). Expectancies, values, and academic behaviors. In J. T. Spence (Ed.), *Achievement and achievement motivation* (pp. 75–146). Freeman.

Eccles, J. S., & Wigfield, A. (1995). In the mind of the actor: The structure of adolescents' achievement task values and expectancy-related beliefs. *Personality and Social Psychology Bulletin, 21*(3), 215–225.

Fokkens-Bruinsma, M., & Canrinus, E. T. (2014). Motivation for becoming a teacher and engagement with the profession: Evidence from different contexts. *International Journal of Educational Research, 65*, 65–74.

Gao, Z., & Chang, B.-N. (2014). Mianfei shifansheng jiaoyu cunzai de wenti jiqi duice yanjiu [Problems and countermeasures in the education of tuition-free normal students]. *Guo Jia Jiao Yu Xing Zheng Xue Yuan Xue Bao, 7*, 31–35.

General Office of the State Council of China. (2007). *Jiaoyubu zhishu shifan daxue shifansheng mianfei jiaoyu shishi banfa [Approaches to implement the Central Government-Funded Teacher Education Policy (Trial) in the six national key teacher-training universities in P.R. China]*. www.gov.cn/zwgk/2007-05/14/content_614039.htm

General Office of the State Council of China. (2018). *Jiaoyubu zhishu shifan daxue shifansheng gongfei jiaoyu shishi banfa [Approaches to implement the Central Government-Funded Teacher Education Policy in the six national key teacher-training universities in P.R. China]*. www.moe.gov.cn/jyb_xxgk/moe_1777/moe_1778/201808/t20180810_345023.html

Graham, S., & Weiner, B. (2012). Motivation: Past, present, and future. In K. R. Harris, S. Graham, T. Urdan, C. B. McCormick, G. M. Sinatra, & J. Sweller (Eds.), *APA educational psychology handbook, Vol 1: Theories, constructs, and critical issues*. American Psychological Association.

Hagger, M. S., & Chatzisarantis, N. L. D. (2011). Causality orientations moderate the undermining effect of rewards on intrinsic motivation. *Journal of Experimental Social Psychology, 47*(2), 485–489.

Jiang, X.-L. (2014). Shifansheng mianfei jiaoyu zhengce de lunli kunjing [Ethical dilemma of the government-funded teacher education policy]. *Gao Jiao Tan Suo, 6*, 43–46.

König, J., & Rothland, M. (2012). Motivations for choosing teaching as a career: Effects on general pedagogical knowledge during initial teacher education. *Asia-Pacific Journal of Teacher Education, 40*(3), 289–315.

Lepper, M. R., Greene, D., & Nisbett, R. E. (1973). Understanding children's intrinsic interest with extrinsic reward: A test of the "overjustification" hypothesis. *Journal of Personality and Social Psychology, 28*(1).

Li, L., Huang, Y.-Y., Xu, X.-C., & Han, Y.-M. (2013). The relationship between entry motivation and professional satisfaction of no-fee preservice students. *Chinese Education & Society, 46*(2), 43–61.

Li, W.-Q. (2007). Guanyu shifansheng mianfei jiaoyu de ruogan sikao [Thoughts on free education for students in teacher education program]. *Jiao Shi Jiao Yu Yan Jiu, 19*(3), 24–28.

Lin, E., Shi, Q.-M., Wang, J., Zhang, S.-A., & Liu, H. (2012). Initial motivations for teaching: Comparison between preservice teachers in the United States and China. *Asia-Pacific Journal of Teacher Education, 40*(3), 227–248.

Lin, G.-Y. (2010). *Education and teacher education in rural areas.* www.pep.com.cn/xgjy/jiaoshi/xsyj/jstd/201008/t20100827_801306.htm

Liu, P. (2010). Examining perspectives of entry-level teacher candidates: A comparative study. *Australian Journal of Teacher Education, 35*(5), 56–78.

Liu, S.-L., Shen, W.-Y., Wang, G.-W., Zhan, Y.-H., Lu, L.-Y., Lu, Z.-S., Zhang, J., Tang, Y., Li, H., Su, Y.-X. (2002). Shifanlei biyesheng jiuye: Huigu yu zhanwang [Employment of pre-service teachers: Retrospect and outlook]. *Zhong Guo Da Xue Sheng Jiu Ye, 10.*

Meece, J. L., Wigfield, A., & Eccles, J. S. (1990). Predictors of math anxiety and its influence on young adolescents' course enrollment intentions and performance in mathematics. *Journal of Educational Psychology, 82*(1), 60.

Mei, X.-L. (Ed.). (2008). *Jujiao zhongguo jiaoshi jiaoyu [Focus on teacher education in China].* Zhong Guo She Hui Ke Xue Chu Ban She.

Murayama, K., Matsumoto, K., Matsumoto, M., Izuma, K., & Smith, E. E. (2010). Neural basis of the undermining effect of monetary reward on intrinsic motivation. *Proceedings of the National Academy of Sciences of the United States of America, 107*(49), 20911–20916.

Paine, L., & Fang, Y.-P. (2009). Dilemmas in reforming China's teaching: Assuring "quality" in professional development. In M. T. Tatto (Ed.), *Reforming teaching globally.* Information Age Publishing Inc.

Peters, K. P., & Vollmer, T. R. (2014). Evaluations of the overjustification effect. *Journal of Behavioral Education, 23*(2), 201–220.

Pittaway, S. M. (2012). Student and staff engagement: Developing an engagement framework in a faculty of education. *Australian Journal of Teacher Education, 37*(4).

Qu, T.-H., & Yuan, Y. (2010). Woguo shifansheng mianfei jiaoyu zhengce de bainian lishi kaocha [Examining the one-hundred-year history of tuition-free teacher education policies in China]. *She Hui Ke Xue Zhan Xian, 175*(1), 213–219.

Richardson, P. W., & Watt, H. M. G. (2010). Current and future directions in teacher motivation research. In T. C. Urdan & S. A. Karabenick (Eds.), *The decade ahead: Applications and contexts of motivation and achievement (Advances in motivation and achievement, Vol. 16)* (pp. 139–173). Emerald Group Publishing Limited.

Richardson, P. W., & Watt, H. M. G. (2014). Why people choose teaching as a career: An expectancy-value approach to understanding teacher motivation. In P. W. Richardson, S. A. Karabenick, & H. M. G. Watt (Eds.), *Teacher motivation: Theory and practice* (pp. 3–19). Routledge.

Roane, H. S., Fisher, W. W., & McDonough, E. M. (2003). Progressing from programmatic to discovery research: A case example with the overjustification effect. *Journal of Applied Behavior Analysis, 36*(1), 35–46.

Schunk, D. H., Pintrich, P. R., & Meece, J. L. (2007). *Motivation in education: Theory, research, and applications.* Pearson Merrill Prentice Hall.

Serow, R. C. (1994). Called to teach: A study of highly motivated preservice teachers. *Journal of Research and Development in Education, 27*(2), 65–72.

Shen, H., & Cai, M. (2019). Gongping jiazhi de yinling: Cong mianfei dao gongfei de shifansheng jiaoyu [Under the guidance of fair value: Education of normal university students from free to publicly-funded]. *Da Xue Jiao Yu Ke Xue, 2,* 66–71.

Song, Y.-G. (2007, May 18). *Jiaoyubu 2007nian diliuci lixing xinwen fabuhui [The sixth press conference in 2007 by the Ministry of Education of P.R. China].* http://edu.people.com.cn/GB/5755241.html

State Council, P. R. C. (1994). Guowuyuan Guanyu "Zhongguo Jiaoyu Gaige He Fazhan Gangyao" De Shishi Yijian [The State Council's Implementation Opinions on "Outline of China's Education Reform and Development"]. *Zhong Hua Ren Min*

16　Background and Rationale for Conducting This Study

Gong He Guo Guo Wu Yuan Gong Bao [Gazette of the State Council of the People's Republic of China](16), 715–730.

Sun, D. (2018). Quanke xiaoxue jiaoshi dingxiang peiyang yanjiu – – mianfei shifan zhengce zhixing de chuangsheng yu gaijin [General teacher training oriented to primary schools: Creation and improvement in carrying out free teacher education policy]. Dong Bei Shi Da Xue Bao (Zhe Xue She Hui Ke Xue Ban), 293(3), 161–165.

Tang, S. H., & Hall, V. C. (1995). The overjustification effect: A meta-analysis. Applied Cognitive Psychology, 9(5), 365–404.

Wang, H. H., & Fwu, B. J. (2001). Why teach? The motivation and commitment of graduate students of a teacher education program in a research university. Proceedings of the National Science Council, 11(4), 390–400.

Wang, T. (Ed.). (1985). Zhongguo dabaike quanshu: Jiaoyu [Encyclopedia of China: Education]. Zhong Guo Da Bai Ke Quan Shu Chu Ban She.

Wang, X., & Niu, X. (2023). Fuquan lilun shijiao xia gongfei shifansheng dui jiaoshi zhiye de renzhi yu xuanze [Government-funded normal university students' cognition and choice of the teaching profession from the perspective of empowerment theory]. Jiao Shi Jiao Yu Xue Bao, 1, 59–68.

Wang, Z.-C. (2011). Shifansheng mianfei jiaoyu zhengce shishi xianzhuang diaocha ji sikao [Investigation and reflection on the implementation of the Central Government-Funded Teacher Education Policy]. Xian Dai Jiao Yu Guan Li, 1.

Wen, J. (2007). Report on the work of the government delivered at the fifth session of the Tenth National People's Congress. The State Council. http://english.gov.cn/official/2007-03/16/content_552995.htm

Wiechman, B. M., & Gurland, S. T. (2009). What happens during the free-choice period? Evidence of a polarizing effect of extrinsic rewards on intrinsic motivation. Journal of Research in Personality, 43(4), 716–719.

Wigfield, A. (1994). Expectancy-value theory of achievement motivation: A developmental perspective. Educational Psychology Review, 6(1), 49–78.

Wigfield, A., & Cambria, J. (2010). Expectancy-value theory: Retrospective and prospective. In T. C. Urdan & S. A. Karabenick (Eds.), The decade ahead: Theoretical perspectives on motivation and achievement (Advances in motivation and achievement Vol. 16 Part A) (pp. 35–70). Emerald Group Publishing Limited.

Wigfield, A., & Eccles, J. S. (1992). The development of achievement task values: A theoretical analysis. Developmental Review, 12(3), 265–310.

Wigfield, A., & Eccles, J. S. (2000). Expectancy-value theory of achievement motivation. Contemporary Educational Psychology, 25(1), 68.

Wong, A. K. Y., Tang, S. Y. F., & Cheng, M. M. H. (2014). Teaching motivations in Hong Kong: Who will choose teaching as a fallback career in a stringent job market? Teaching and Teacher Education, 41, 81–91.

Wu, Z.-M., & Liu, F. (2008). Mianfei shifansheng jiaoyu zhengce chuyi [On the policy of free education for undergraduates in normal universities]. Hang Zhou Shi Fan Da Xue Xue Bao (She Hui Ke Xue Ban), 6.

Zhang, L. (2007, March 6). Shifansheng mianfei jiaoyu de "huigui" zhilu [The journey of returning back to no-fee teacher education]. Jing Hua Shi Bao.

Zhou, Q. (2013). Mianfei shifansheng zhengce renzhi diaocha – yi xinan daxue wei gean [Investigation on the free normal students' cognitive of policy: Take Southwest University as a case]. Jiao Shi Jiao Yu Yan Jiu, 25(3), 60–65.

2 Literature Review

Introduction

This chapter provides a review of the literature on the career-choice motivations of teachers and on the CGFTE policy. The chapter describes the diverse motivations to teach in various countries and regions around the world, in particular attractors and facilitators and intrinsic, extrinsic, and altruistic motivations of teachers' career choices. The chapter includes discussions of multiple factors that could influence teachers' choice of the teaching profession, including gender, family background, and teacher education. Moreover, the chapter examines themes and trends of research on the CGFTE policy and its influence on pre-service teachers' career-choice motivations. Through this literature review, gaps in the research areas are identified, and the significance of the present study is discussed.

2.1 Teachers' Career-Choice Motivations

The question of why individuals choose to teach has been extensively explored, with an increasing number of studies on this topic in recent decades. These studies have been diverse in terms of research contexts and participants' demographic backgrounds. This section reviews studies guided by three main questions: (i) What are teachers' primary career-choice motivations, and how important are they? (ii) How can we classify teachers' career-choice motivations? and (iii) What factors influence teachers' career-choice motivations?

2.1.1 Teachers' Career-Choice Motivation Profiles in Different Contexts

Teaching is a career that varies significantly in terms of rewards and demands across countries. These differences, along with the diversity of employment situations, economies, societies, cultures, policies, and traditions of the countries, can shape teachers' career-choice motivations. Therefore, researchers have explored teachers' career-choice motivations from many specific countries, districts, or other areas.

DOI: 10.4324/9781032639680-2

18 *Literature Review*

Studies on the career-choice motivation of teachers in the United States have a long history. Authors of an early study found that American high school students who aspired to teach were less concerned about earning a high salary than were those who planned to pursue other careers (Roberson et al., 1983). A qualitative study conducted by Su (1993) on American teacher candidates, based on national research project data, showed that they chose teaching because they enjoyed working with children and young people, liked working with people, wanted to serve others, had interests in the subject area, and needed compatibility between teaching and family life. American school students with interests in teaching listed their top three motives as knowledge and skills in the subject they would teach, a desire to work with young people, and interests in the chosen subject, whereas salary, job availability, and reputation were their last three motives (Summerhill et al., 1998). A systematic review of studies published from 2002 to 2006 on the recruitment and retention of teachers in America concluded that American pre-service teachers were more motivated to teach by intrinsic reasons such as "helping children and young people" than extrinsic factors such as "job security or pay", and the two most commonly cited reasons for wanting to teach in America were "wanting to work with children" and "having a high regard for the teaching profession" (Bielby et al., 2007, p. 4).

Multiple researchers have explored the career-choice motivations of teachers in other advanced economies, including Australia (Richardson & Watt, 2006; Sinclair, 2008), New Zealand (Lovett, 2007), the United Kingdom (Ivan & Jonathan, 1997), Ireland (Heinz, 2013; Moran et al., 2001), the Netherlands (Fokkens-Bruinsma & Canrinus, 2012, 2014), Germany (König & Rothland, 2012), Greece (Doliopoulou, 1995), and Singapore (Goh & Atputhasamy, 2001; Low et al., 2011). These researchers' studies have generally revealed similar results to those found in America.

In Australia, Richardson and Watt (2006) developed and validated a scale to measure pre-service teachers' motivation to teach and found that perceived competency in teaching, intrinsic value of teaching, and working with children were the highest-ranked motivations, and teaching as a fallback career and following others' suggestions were the least important. Sinclair (2008) conducted another study on Australian first-year pre-service teachers and found that their motivations to become primary teachers were multifaceted. The most important reasons for choosing teaching were self-evaluation about their characteristics and abilities suitable for teaching, loving working with children, and the intellectual challenge of teaching. Lovett (2007) conducted a qualitative study in New Zealand and found that working with children and making a difference in their development were the dominant motivational factors for promising teachers. The study also revealed no significant difference in career-choice motivation between the first-career teachers and the career changers (Lovett, 2007).

In the United Kingdom, Ivan and Jonathan (1997) found that 96% of preservice teachers were motivated to enter the Postgraduate Certificate in Education mainly by intrinsic and altruistic factors, such as enjoying working with youth and experiencing high job satisfaction. In Northern Ireland, Moran et al. (2001) found that teacher candidates selected teaching mainly for intrinsic reasons, although there were also extrinsic motives. In a later study, Heinz (2013) found that Irish pre-service teachers chose teaching with high altruistic incentives, such as making a social contribution, shaping the future generation, and commitment to teaching, that were balanced by realistic perspectives, such as the high difficulty of the teaching profession and the relatively low social status and salary for teachers. In the Netherlands, researchers using the FIT-Choice scale found that intrinsic motivations such as self-perceived teaching abilities (Fokkens-Bruinsma & Canrinus, 2012) and working with children and adolescents (Fokkens-Bruinsma & Canrinus, 2014) were the most important reasons for Dutch pre-service teachers to choose teaching. Social influences and perceiving teaching as a useful career were reported as the least important motivations (Fokkens-Bruinsma & Canrinus, 2012). In Germany, König and Rothland (2012) replicated the typical motivational characteristics of pre-service teachers. Working with children was rated as the most important motivation, followed by other factors such as the intrinsic value of teaching, shaping the future, perceived competency in teaching, and contributing to society. Doliopoulou (1995) conducted a study in Greece and found that female kindergarten teacher candidates had chosen teaching primarily because they loved working with children.

In Singapore, Goh and Atputhasamy (2001) showed that the most popular motives for pre-service teachers to choose teaching were fondness for teaching and working with children, the ability to positively influence others' lives, and teaching as an intellectually stimulating and noble job, which were all altruistic in nature. Low et al. (2011) identified nine reasons for Singaporean pre-service teachers to choose teaching categorised into three broad clusters, altruistic, intrinsic, and extrinsic, and found altruistic and intrinsic motivations in 96% of the sample. Moreover, in a series of early studies in Singapore (e.g., Lau, 1968; Soh, 1989), the predominant factors motivating student teachers to enter the teaching profession were intrinsic and altruistic, such as serving society, developing the young, and fondness for children.

Researchers have conducted a comparatively small number of studies on the career-choice motivations of teachers in developing countries. In one early study, Olaseboye Olasehinde (1972) in Nigeria found that "nothing else to do" was the second most important motive for primary teachers' career choice (p. 209). Later, teaching quality, dressing style, and teachers' communicating capability were the most influential motivations for Nigerian senior secondary school students to choose teaching (Adkintomide & Oluwatosin, 2011). In Zimbabwe, salary, fringe benefits, and working conditions had the greatest influence on the attractiveness of a teaching career for pre-service teachers (Chivore, 1988). In Jamaica, Evans (1993) found that 55% of interviewees (newly graduated teacher trainees) were forced into teacher-training colleges by their personal circumstances, such as blocked aspirations and easy entry to teacher college, but in a later study, extrinsic motivations, such as many holidays, cheap college fees, and time compatibility, were the most significant reasons Jamaican teacher candidates chose teaching as a career (Bastick, 2000). In Brunei Darussalam, Yong (1995) found that "no other choice" and "influence of others", extrinsic factors, were the two most important reasons for teacher trainees in that country to choose teaching as a career (p. 276). For Turkish pre-service English teachers, social utility, intrinsic value, and ability-related beliefs were the top three motivational factors for choosing teaching as their future career (Topkaya & Uztosun, 2012). Teaching motivations were found to be diversified for pre-service teachers from different teacher-training programs in Indonesia. Specifically, early childhood and special education participants entered the program because they wanted to enhance social equity, primary education participants were more motivated by their teaching ability and intrinsic value, and English language education participants were the least motivated (Suryani, 2021).

Comparing the research findings listed above reveals dissimilarities among countries in terms of the primary motivations for choosing the teaching profession. Teachers from advanced economies tend to choose teaching for altruistic and intrinsic reasons, whereas their counterparts from developing countries are more attracted to extrinsic benefits. For instance, an early comparative study by Papanastasiou and Papanastasiou (1997) showed that pre-service teachers from Cyprus were highly motivated by extrinsic factors such as "variety of benefits" and "status of the profession" (p. 305) to enter initial teacher preparation programs. In contrast, the strongest factor that influenced their American counterparts was intrinsic motives. In a subsequent study, Bastick (2000) analysed existing research findings and found that teacher students from developing countries generally emphasised extrinsic motivations whereas those from metropolitan countries emphasised intrinsic and altruistic motivations. These differences suggest that socio-cultural contexts could shape teachers' career-choice motivations (e.g., Bastick, 2000; Richardson & Watt, 2010). However, these studies' findings are culturally specific to western and other non-Chinese societies.

In the Chinese context, teachers usually exhibit "complex and nested" (Gu & Lai, 2012, pp. 47–48), changeable (Tang et al., 2014), and even ambivalent (Cheng et al., 2015) motives for choosing the teaching profession. In a large-scale national study, Su et al. (2001) surveyed around 2,000 pre-service teachers and 400 teacher educators from 23 teacher-training institutions in mainland China and found that the young participants did not rate teaching as a lucrative or popular profession; instead, Chinese pre-service teachers disliked teaching as a career because of the low social status, hard work, and low salary. The teachers also complained about the slowly increasing salary for teachers, high inflation rates, and low availability of school housing, which revealed the comparatively low social and economic status of teaching (Su et al., 2001). In Hong Kong SAR, most pre-service teachers' motivations were intrinsic (Tang et al., 2015), and in Macau SAR, pre-service teachers were highly motivated to improve the teaching and learning situation in the region and bring positive changes to its educational context (Yu, 2015). In fact, pre-service teachers from Macau SAR and Hong Kong SAR share commonality in their altruistic and intrinsic motivations (Tang et al., 2018). In a recent study, researchers found that Chinese pre-service teachers generally exhibit a high degree of motivation for teaching (Ye et al., 2022).

In analysing autobiographical writings and in-depth interviews of four experienced or retired Chinese mainland teachers, Li and Niyozov (2008) found that the teachers' career choices were significantly impacted by the reversing educational policy and the changing Chinese society during the last decades of the 20th century. Chinese teachers' professional identities were constantly shaped and reshaped by social realities and forces, including the Cultural Revolution (1966–1976), the Reform and Open-Door Policy (1978), and the changing foreign language education policy since 1949. The authors found limited autonomy for Chinese teachers' professional choices at that time, when "the state's preference, rather than personal and professional needs, determined what one would do" (Li & Niyozov, 2008, p. 78). Taking foreign language teachers for example, instead of resisting actively, they tended to follow the Chinese Taoist principle to "reconstruct themselves to meet the changing foreign language teaching policies in China" (Li & Niyozov, 2008, p. 77).

Several researchers explored why Chinese mainland teachers chose to teach English (e.g., Gao & Trent, 2009; Zhao, 2008). For instance, Zhao (2008) used the life-history narrative approach to explore 17 Chinese teachers' motivation to teach English in secondary schools in mainland China, and four themes about their career-choice motivations emerged: entering the teaching profession without making a conscious decision, enjoying teaching the subject of English, the sense of security provided by the teaching job, and wanting to influence people. However, authors of a different qualitative study did not identify any of these themes in their study of the experiences of ten Chinese mainland pre-service English teachers at a teacher-education program in Hong Kong SAR (Gao & Trent, 2009). Rather, the students' motivations to enrol in English teacher-education programs were mainly extrinsic, such as teaching job security, the prestige of teaching a foreign language, and acquiring transferable skills including English proficiency (Gao & Trent, 2009). This finding was echoed in a later study in which pre-service teachers from the Chinese mainland regarded the availability of English-learning opportunities and the opportunity for self-development in non-teaching occupations as important reasons to attend teacher-training institutions in Hong Kong (Gu & Lai, 2012). Li et al. (2013) examined entry motivations to teacher-education programs among 612 student teachers supported by the CGFTE policy and found that four factors motivated the students to enrol in these programs: their perceptions of the teaching profession; the attractive provisions in the programs; intrinsic values of teaching; and social influences from teachers, parents, and friends.

Literature also compares motivation to teach between the Chinese mainland and other contexts, such as the USA and Hong Kong SAR. An earlier comparative study by Su et al. (2001) on pre-service teachers' choice and commitment to teaching between the Chinese mainland and the USA showed that both Chinese and American pre-service teachers generally emphasised intrinsic reasons more than extrinsic reasons for choosing teaching. However, Su et al. found several unique features of Chinese pre-service teachers' motivations. When compared with their American counterparts, the Chinese pre-service teachers rated intrinsic reasons lower and extrinsic reasons higher. Furthermore, mainly due to the low social status and poor benefits of teaching in China, most Chinese pre-service teachers did not intend to stay lifelong in the teaching profession, although they regarded teaching as a noble career similar to their American counterparts (Su et al., 2001).

In another comparative study, Liu (2010) found that Chinese and American pre-service teachers shared similar views on the role of teachers but had notable differences in their motivations to teach and perceived accomplishments as future teachers. Through analysing informants' written responses on motivation to teach, Liu found that the most popular reasons for Chinese pre-service teachers to choose teaching as a future career were the security and nobility of teaching, scores on university entrance exams, the desire and opportunity to educate the future generation, and the long breaks inherent to teaching jobs. The Chinese pre-service teachers were not primarily driven by their intrinsic motivation to choose teaching but rather by extrinsic factors such as lower scores on university entrance exams, responsibility to serve society, social status of teachers, tuition waivers in teacher-training programs, and other advantages of teaching (Liu, 2010). In comparison, the most popular motivations for American pre-service teachers to choose teaching were making a difference, personal interest and passion, previous teachers' influence, intrinsic rewards, and a love for working with children (Liu, 2010). In short, whereas American pre-service teachers were mainly attracted to the teaching profession by their passion for teaching and working with children, their Chinese counterparts were more motivated by extrinsic factors (Liu, 2010).

In a later comparative study, Lin et al. (2012) administered the FIT-Choice scale and found that Chinese and American pre-service teachers had both similarities and differences in their career-choice motivations and perceptions about teaching. Both cohorts of pre-service teachers emphasised the social value of teaching and perceived teaching as a profession with low social status (Lin et al., 2012). However, when compared with their American counterparts, Chinese pre-service teachers were less motivated to become teachers by the social value of teaching, personal teaching capacity, personal interests in teaching, and previous educating experience (Lin et al., 2012). Instead, they were more motivated by fallback factors, such as being unsure of career goals and being refused their first-choice career; moreover, Chinese pre-service teachers regarded teaching as a less demanding career and were less satisfied with their choice of teaching than their American counterparts (Lin et al., 2012).

Similar intrinsic, altruistic, and extrinsic motives were found by Gu and Lai (2012) for Chinese pre-service teachers from the Chinese mainland and Hong Kong SAR to enrol in a teacher-education program. The intrinsic and altruistic motivations included love for children and shaping individuals' lives through teaching, whereas the extrinsic reasons were mainly related to the advantages of teaching in Hong Kong SAR, such as job security, lengthy holidays, decent salary, and a relatively less competitive working environment (Gu & Lai, 2012). However, two unique motives were noted for Chinese mainland pre-service teachers: the English-speaking context in Hong Kong SAR and personal development opportunities provided by the teaching vocation (Gu & Lai, 2012).

2.1.2 Categories of Career-Choice Motivations of Teachers

The actions people take, including making a career choice, are usually motivated by multiple concerns. Although numerous studies have produced fact-based results on the career-choice motivations of teachers in different contexts, some researchers have focused on conceptually analysing these diverse motivations (Ferrell & Daniel, 1993). This study reviews two frameworks for classifying teaching career choice motivations based on the literature consulted.

2.1.2.1 Attractors and Facilitators

This framework is derived from an early study conducted by Lortie (1975), who made a significant effort to explain why people enter teaching. Lortie collected data from intensive interviews with in-service teachers in five towns in the Boston metropolitan area from the early 1960s to the early 1970s. The author also consulted data from National Education Association national surveys. Lortie published the findings of this seminal study in the book *Schoolteacher*. In the second chapter of the book, Lortie summarises and adapts an early framework for classifying teachers' career-choice motivations, namely into the two broad domains of attractors and facilitators (pp. 25–54). Attractors refer to the various comparative advantages people can gain if they choose teaching as a career, and facilitators refer to the less noticeable social mechanisms that propel individuals into teaching.

There are five categories of attractors: interpersonal, service, continuation, material benefits, and time compatibility. Interpersonal attractors relate to the opportunities teaching provides for working with the youth. One unique feature of a teaching career, as described by Lortie (1975), is that "it

24 Literature Review

calls for protracted contact with young people" (p. 27). Individuals who are keen to work with children and have the desire to maintain steady interaction with them could be attracted to a teaching career for these interpersonal reasons. The second category, service, reflects that in cultures that respect those who fulfil a special and sacred mission for society, such as American culture, a teaching career can be more attractive than other occupations (Lortie, 1975).

Continuation as an attractor to a teaching career relates to people who enjoy school environments and feel it is difficult to engage in other contexts; "school-linked pursuits" (Lortie, 1975, p. 29) attract them to continue working in schools. For the last two attractors, material benefits mean the rewards of teaching, such as income, prestige, and employment security, and time compatibility refers to the flexibility of teachers' working schedules, which can be compatible with family life (Lortie, 1975). Both play a role in attracting people to the teaching profession.

There are also four categories of facilitators. "Wide decision range" means that individuals can decide to become teachers at several points in their lives, which could facilitate expanding the pool of potential teaching force (Lortie, 1975). "Subjective warrant" refers to individuals' justifications for choosing teaching based on self-judgment of their personality, interests, capabilities, etc. (Lortie, 1975). The next category, "early and affective decisions", denotes the choice of a teaching career at an early age due to identification with appropriate teacher models and/or reinforcement by a supportive environment; this often happens to "marginal students" (Lortie, 1975, p. 43) who are experiencing different cultures and can be easily influenced by teachers and to family members who follow the teaching occupation of their parents or other kin. It can also happen when individuals are labelled by their significant others, such as parents, friends, and colleagues (Lortie, 1975). Lastly, "entry under constraint" means that teaching is chosen as a career as a result of some restrictions, which include socio-economic limitations, unavailability of expensive college education, parental interventions, obstacles to original ambition and convertibility, and disadvantages of previous careers (Lortie, 1975).

Lortie's (1975) classification of motivations for choosing teaching as a career inspired further discussions in many studies (e.g., Ferrell & Daniel, 1993; Joseph & Green, 1986; Low et al., 2011; H. H. Wang & Fwu, 2001). In the study conducted by Joseph and Green (1986), additional motivational factors such as "stimulation", "influence of others", and "psychological" (p. 29) were added to Lortie's framework. In another study, researchers statistically tested and refined Lortie's framework (Ferrell & Daniel, 1993). Based on Lortie's teaching motivation framework, Wang and Fwu (2001) applied attractors and facilitators, along with exploration, parenting, and knowledge, as the five categories of teaching motivations.

2.1.2.2 Intrinsic, Extrinsic, and Altruistic Factors

Many researchers have used empirical approaches to investigate the career-choice motivations of teachers in various contexts, following the classical study of Lortie (1975). Teacher motivations are diverse and complex, and researchers who focus on specific participant groups often categorise their motivations into different types. However, despite the varied contexts, numerous studies suggest that certain types of motivation are prevalent among teachers' career choices.

Brookhart and Freeman (1992) found that pre-service teachers frequently cited "altruistic, service-oriented goals, and other intrinsic sources of motivation" (p. 46) as major reasons for choosing a teaching career. Moran et al. (2001) classified motivational factors into two groups – intrinsic and extrinsic reasons – based on empirical results. This is consistent with Wang and Fwu's (2001) suggestion that people are generally attracted to the teaching profession for two sets of reasons: intrinsic factors closely associated with the nature and conditions of the job and extrinsic factors that drive one to choose teaching as a career. Following Lortie's (1975) work, the classification of "extrinsic, intrinsic, and altruistic" motivations for choosing a teaching career has been widely adopted in many studies (e.g., Chan, 2006; Kyriacou et al., 1999; Low et al., 2011; Roness, 2011; Sinclair et al., 2006; Thomson et al., 2012; Topkaya & Uztosun, 2012; Williams & Forgasz, 2009; Younger et al., 2004). Bastick (2000) verified an EIA factor model through factor analysis in Jamaica.

Kyriacou and his colleagues examined and emphasised the descriptive definitions of extrinsic, intrinsic, and altruistic teaching career choice motivations in a series of studies published from the late 1990s to the early 2000s (Kobori & Kyriacou, 1998; Kyriacou & Benmansour, 1999; Kyriacou & Coulthard, 2000; Kyriacou et al., 1999). As concluded by Kyriacou and Coulthard (2000), the three motivational categories can be described as follows: altruistic motives involve seeing teaching as a socially worthwhile and important job, a desire to help children succeed, and a desire to help society improve; intrinsic motives cover aspects of the job activity itself, such as teaching children and utilising one's subject matter knowledge and expertise; and extrinsic motives cover aspects of the job that are not inherent in the work itself, such as long holidays, level of pay, and status (p. 117).

Understandings of the relationships among the three types of teaching career choice motivation are diverse. Early studies often viewed the different motivations, such as intrinsic versus extrinsic, as incompatible (Deci & Ryan, 2000). A later study (Covington & Müeller, 2001) suggested a bipolar or unidimensional model of motivation, where extrinsic and intrinsic motives blended within an individual who could be dominated by one motivational factor. Similarly, Moran et al. (2001) emphasised that not everyone exhibited all three types of motivation when considering teaching as a career choice and found different motivations in particular between female and male teacher candidates in general. In a study applying the typological approach, Thomson et al. (2012) found that every participant expressed a combination of different altruistic, intrinsic, and extrinsic teaching motivations to some degree, and none reported only one type of motivation. Additionally, through a literature review, Low et al. (2011) proposed that

> the diverse taxonomy of motivations, uncovered by numerous studies, dovetail with one another; the intrinsic, extrinsic and altruistic categories very much reflect the attractors, while personal influences that are featured in many articles resonate with the facilitators described by Lortie.
>
> (p. 196)

2.1.3 Factors Influencing the Choice of Teaching

The career-choice motivations of teachers are full of complexities and paradoxes (Zhao, 2008). In the process of choosing a teaching career, motivation and demotivation factors coexist (Dörnyei & Ushioda, 2011; Hatch, 1999). When individuals choose teaching as their future career, they may or may not have the "free choice" of their desired career as "they may be constrained by internal and external resources" (Richardson & Watt, 2010, p. 142). Factors related to gender, family background, teacher education, and other variables can influence teachers' career-choice motivation, as drawn from the literature.

2.1.3.1 Gender

Teaching is often viewed as a "woman's work" due to its reputation as a stable profession (e.g., Edmonds et al., 2002; Goodson & Hargreaves, 1996; Hatch, 1999; Zhao, 2008), and the phenomenon of women teaching while men manage (Rury, 1986) was once pervasive. Female teachers were found to be more child-centred (e.g., Brookhart & Freeman, 1992; Drudy & Ebooks, 2005; Heinz, 2013) and to have a stronger affinity for the teaching profession (Su et al., 2001), whereas male teachers had stronger aspirations for running a school and having a great influence on education (Wang & Fwu, 2001).

Findings from studies conducted in various countries reveal that the number of female pre-service teachers in teacher-training programs exceeds that of their male counterparts (e.g., Guarino et al., 2006; Richardson & Watt, 2006; Z.-X. Su et al., 2001). This unbalanced proportion has attracted the attention of many researchers globally to explore the influences of gender on pre-service teachers' career-choice motivation. One common finding is that female pre-service teachers tend to place greater importance on intrinsic reasons for choosing teaching, while male pre-service teachers tend to emphasise extrinsic career-choice motivations. Moran et al. (2001) found gender differences in motivation to teach among Northern Ireland pre-service teachers. Female pre-service teachers attached greater importance than males to intrinsic motivations, such as enjoying working with children, having a sense of mission, experiencing intellectual challenge, and making a social contribution. Moreover, females rejected the influence of the factor "teacher training and teaching as employment" more strongly than males (Moran et al., 2001, p. 23). Authors of another study in Ireland found that compared with their male counterparts, female pre-service teachers attached greater importance to "working with children" as their motivation to teach, and their decision to teach was significantly influenced by previous teaching and learning experiences (Heinz, 2013). In the context of Chinese societies, similar research findings were reached. In a study with participants of 1,249 students from 20 Hong Kong SAR secondary schools, approximately 55% of female students expressed interest in teaching (Lai et al., 2005). In another study, when compared with male counterparts, female pre-service teachers were found to be more motivated by the CGFTE policy, the intrinsic value of the teaching profession, and their perceptions of the profession (Li et al., 2013).

However, not all studies have found significant differences in motivation to teach between male and female pre-service teachers. For example, in a survey approach study conducted in Singapore, there were no significant differences between male and female teacher candidates in any of the motive factors, which suggested that they were attracted to the teaching career for the same reasons (Goh & Atputhasamy, 2001). Similar findings were reported in the study conducted by Richardson and Watt (2005), who found very little evidence for gender differences in the career-choice motivations of pre-service teachers at an Australian university.

2.1.3.2 Family Background

In general, pre-service teachers come from families with lower incomes than those of other university students (e.g., Brookhart & Freeman, 1992; Richardson & Watt, 2006; Z.-X. Su et al., 2001; Wu et al., 2022). Some studies explore the influence of family background on pre-service teachers' career-choice motivation. In the study conducted by Lai et al. (2005), the results showed that secondary school students in Hong Kong SAR from higher-income families were less interested in teaching than those from lower-income families, indicating that teaching was a less attractive career option for students from relatively wealthy families. Another study (Li et al., 2013) found that the family economic status of Chinese pre-service teachers could be related to their entry motivation into government-funded teacher-education programs. Those with higher family income generally placed greater importance on the attractiveness of the CGFTE policy as their motivation to enter teacher-education programs; however, their counterparts with lower family income cited social persuasion as a more important motivational factor.

2.1.3.3 Teacher Education

Teacher education, particularly the teacher-training program, is often criticised for failing to familiarise pre-service teachers with future teaching experiences, creating a gap between the theories they were taught at university and the practical problems they encounter in the classroom (e.g., Cochran-Smith & Zeichner, 2005; Darling-Hammond et al., 2001). Nevertheless, some investigators have explored the potential influences of teacher education on pre-service teachers' career-choice motivation and development (Shak, 2022).

Sinclair et al. (2006) presumed that career-choice motivations of pre-service teachers could be shaped by real-life experiences gained from a teaching internship during teacher preparation. This assumption was supported by a later study (Sinclair, 2008) in which some changes in motivation to teach were primarily due to the influence of the first-year teaching practicum. In comparing first-year and last-year pre-service teachers in a one-year training program in the Netherlands, Fokkens-Bruinsma and Canrinus (2012) found that social influence and teaching ability were more important teaching motivations by those at the end of the program than among their counterparts at the beginning stage. In their later study, the teaching motives of Netherlandish pre-service teachers generally remained stable, but "social utility value" as their teaching career choice motivation was rated significantly lower at the end of teacher education (Canrinus & Fokkens-Bruinsma, 2014).

2.1.3.4 Other Factors

The diversity of motives people report for choosing to teach is believed to be influenced by the social and cultural contexts in which they are involved (Kyriacou et al., 1999). Teaching is often described as a secure and reputable career (Cavanagh, 2007) and is highly regarded in Chinese traditional culture, acting as a promoting factor for many Chinese pre-service teachers to choose teaching (Liu, 2010). Similarly, Australian pre-service teachers are attracted to the teaching profession because of the high status of teachers among other factors (Sinclair, 2008). A comparative study revealed that the career-choice motivation of Canadian pre-service teachers focused more on individual and social value utilities, whereas Omani counterparts were more influenced by social culture and more likely to choose teaching as a fallback career (Klassen et al., 2011).

Multiple researchers have explored the influence of major subjects on the choice of the teaching profession. In one study, Hong Kong SAR secondary school students in art streams were more interested in teaching than were those in science or commerce (Lai et al., 2005). When compared with their counterparts majoring in science and humanities, Chinese pre-service teachers in the majors of drawing, music, and physical education rated social influences higher and their perceptions about teaching lower among their motivations for entering a teacher-training program (Li et al., 2013).

However, some factors are likely to decrease motivation to choose teaching as a career, according to Gordon (2000), who studied Asian minority students in America. These resistant factors include parental pressure for positions with higher social status and financial rewards, high requirements of Chinese culture for teachers, and concerns about uncomfortable work in the educational environment (Gordon, 2000).

2.2 Studies on the Central Government-Funded Teacher Education Policy

Since its implementation in September 2007, the CGFTE policy has continuously attracted the attention of educational researchers. Issues related to the CGFTE policy have become one of the most popular topics in the field of educational policy research (Sun, 2011), and an increasing number of studies on this policy have been conducted in recent years.

2.2.1 Research Themes and Trends

Studies on the CGFTE policy have shown some trends and research themes (e.g., Di et al., 2022; Ma & Cui, 2017; Sun & Chu, 2008; Sun, 2011; Wang et al., 2013; Zhao, 2012). Those published before 2008 mainly discussed the reasons for and significance of launching this policy, measures for implementing it, and expectations about its outcomes (Sun & Chu, 2008). From 2007 to 2010, scholars tended to analyse the significance of the policy and provide information on how to improve it; however, few examined the consequences and effects brought about by implementing the policy (Sun, 2011). Moreover, master's degree theses related to this policy conducted in 2009 and 2010 mainly explored two themes: one was the learning attitudes, initiatives, and motivation of PFPTs; the other was their professional identity and professional satisfaction (Li et al., 2013). According to the findings of a comprehensive review of related studies published from 2007 to 2012 (Wang et al., 2013), research topics focused on PFPTs' employment, professional identity, curriculum provision, and the development of this CGFTE policy.

Additionally, a review focusing on methodology concluded that the major research methods applied in those studies included discourse analysis, historical analysis, and quantitative research (Zhao, 2012). From the perspective of discourse analysis, two concepts were proposed to name the policy: "government-funded teacher education policy" and "free teacher education policy". By historical analysis, researchers argued for dividing China's teacher education into both historical and social political points of view. In the studies that applied quantitative methods, researchers analysed psychological characteristics and perceptions of PFPTs. Zhao (2012) argued that the concept of "government-funded teacher education policy" was more appropriate and clearer than "free teacher education policy" and suggested that future researchers should adopt structured content analyses and comprehensive research methods to deepen people's understanding of this policy. In recent studies, Liu and Li (2022) found that the proportion of PFPTs willing to teach was significantly higher than that of self-sponsored pre-service teachers, and Di et al. (2022) revealed that the teachers who graduated from universities carrying out the CGFTE policy did not improve students' academic performance as much as other teachers, probably because of the negative incentives of the policy.

2.2.2 Career-Choice Motivations of Policy-Funded Pre-service Teachers

Some researchers have explored issues closely related to the career-choice motivations of PFPTs, such as their motivations to enter government-funded teacher-training programs (e.g., Li, 2010, 2011; Li et al., 2013; Liu, 2009; Wang, 2011; Yao et al., 2012; Zhang & Zhao, 2016; Zhou, 2013) and their teaching-profession identity (e.g., Fan, 2010; Feng et al., 2010; Pan & Wang, 2020; Zhao et al., 2011). According to the findings, PFPTs' motivations to choose teacher-training programs are diverse. Among them, the most significant motive factors included waived and compensated university fees and costs, guaranteed employment, and teaching dreams (Li, 2010, 2011; Zhou, 2013).

Regarding receiving funding for university fees and costs, a study (Li, 2011) found that male teacher students rated this motivation significantly higher than did their female counterparts, and those from rural-area families rated it significantly higher than those from urban areas. Based on their survey of PFPTs from all six teacher-training universities implementing the CGFTE policy, Yao and Dong (2009) concluded that the family incomes of PFPTs had significant impacts on their motivation to enrol in government-funded teacher-training programs; for instance, those with poor family backgrounds usually placed a high emphasis on tuition-free education and ignored their personal interest and aspiration in teaching when deciding to enrol in the programs. Authors of a later study (Yao et al., 2012) found that the PFPTs' enrolment motives were significantly related to their family economic conditions and household registrations, and with the increase in years of study at university, the economic reasons for choosing the teaching profession became more significant, while their teaching aspirations became weaker. Therefore, Yao et al. (2012) suggested that CGFTE universities reform their teacher-training curricula to enhance the professionalisation of pre-service teachers. Different from these views, some researchers (Li et al., 2013) found that although the provisions about tuition waiving and employment guarantee in the CGFTE policy had great attraction for many students from rural families where parents usually had low income and low social status but great concerns for their children's employment after graduation, the economic benefits of the policy were not the most important reason for the PFPTs to choose the teacher-training programs of the universities carrying out the policy.

Studies (e.g., Feng et al., 2010; Liu, 2009) have found that the teacher professional identity of PFPTs is generally positive and strong. Through pursuing the teaching profession, PFPTs hope to achieve professional aspiration, strengthen personal interest, and maintain harmonious family relationship (Feng et al., 2010), but they are not satisfied with school leadership, teaching environment, asnd teachers' salary (Liu, 2009; Pan & Wang, 2020). Through interviews with teacher educators and college advisors, Fan (2010) concluded that PFPTs face problems such as feeling uncertain about their future career development, worrying about the low income of the teaching profession, lack of learning motivation, and having low self-confidence. Based on empowerment theory and interview data from 42 PFPTs, Wang and Niu (2023) believed that the cognition and choice of the teaching profession for the PFPTs is the empowerment process, which includes facing a weak power condition, self-awareness awakening, actively seeking dialogue, gaining a teacher's professional meaning, and independently choosing to teach.

In another study, Zhao et al. (2011) proposed a three-dimensional model and confirmed it for measuring PFPTs' teacher professional identities. The three dimensions were intrinsic value identity (e.g., personal interest in teaching, sense of professional value, sense of achievement through teaching), extrinsic value identity (e.g., teachers' salary, social status of teaching, and working conditions), and volitional behaviour identity (e.g., paying attention to educational policies, reading books about teachers and teaching, and attending teacher-training activities) (Zhao et al., 2011). According to the quantitative results of the study, the PFPTs had stronger intrinsic than extrinsic value identities, and volitional behaviour identity was the lowest; moreover, female PFPTs had stronger professional identity in every dimension of the model than did the men, and the PFPTs' rating of their teaching identity gradually decreased with more years of study at university (Zhao et al., 2011).

2.3 Summary and Reflection

This chapter reviewed studies in two content areas: teachers' career-choice motivations and the CGFTE policy in the Chinese mainland. Various issues under each content area relevant to the current study were discussed, and some research gaps were revealed.

The review of studies on teachers' career-choice motivation reflects that research in this content area has experienced some changes in the past half-century regarding methodology and focus. Early studies were mainly empirical reports that explored motivation profiles of specific contexts using relatively small-scale diversified surveys. However, as Wang and Fwu (2001) noted, one of the shortcomings in this field was that few studies probed into the complex and dynamic process of how individuals developed their motivations to teach. Therefore, in-depth and dynamic approaches to explore the underlying motives of promising students to teach were needed. These approaches included applying in-depth open-ended interviews as the method of inquiry (Corbin & Strauss, 1990; Glaser & Strauss, 1968). In later studies, cross-context designs and qualitative inquiries gradually attracted researchers' interest and were applied by some researchers.

Current teacher motivation research seems to have entered a new era where theoretically grounded instruments, such as the FIT-Choice scale, have been developed and validated in different contexts. International comparative studies have become feasible and popular, and both quantitative and qualitative approaches are applied to explore the complexity and richness of teacher motivation. Meanwhile, researchers' interest has expanded beyond exploring motivation profiles to probing correlations between teaching motivation and other related areas such as teaching commitment, job satisfaction, and professional development.

However, most researchers have explored the relationship between pre-service teachers' career-choice motivation and their "planned" factors related to future classroom teaching (e.g., Losh & Wilke, 2008; Saban, 2003). As few of them conducted longitudinal follow-ups, these findings are still open to questions that can only be tested when those pre-service teachers become in-service teachers. Moreover, it appears that some significant questions, such as "how we can influence the motivation for becoming a teacher" (Fokkens-Bruinsma & Canrinus, 2014, p. 73), have not been addressed in existing studies.

The review of studies on the CGFTE policy reveals that few researchers directly explored the career-choice motivations of the PFPTs. Moreover, none explored the impacts of the CGFTE policy on the career-choice motivations of PFPTs. The present study aims to reduce these deficits to some degree. As some early psychological studies indicated that motivation was able to promote school students' continuing and useful engagement in a task or activity (Ames, 1992; Barker et al., 2002), the findings of the present study are expected to shed light on understanding the effects of pre-service teachers' career-choice motivation on their study engagement at the university-based teacher education level. Moreover, the research purpose of the present study is to explore the impacts brought about by the CGFTE policy on pre-service teachers' career-choice motivation. No similar studies were found in this literature review. The results of the present study are, therefore, expected to add some evidence to fill the gap existing in the current literature about how the CGFTE policy influences teachers' career-choice motivations.

References

Adkintomide, A. G., & Oluwatosin, S. A. (2011). Teacher characteristics and students' choice of teaching as a career in Osun state. *Edo Journal of Counselling, 4*(1–2), 116–129.

Ames, C. (1992). Classrooms: Goals, structures, and student motivation. *Journal of Educational Psychology*, *84*(3), 261–271.
Barker, K. L., McInerney, D. M., & Dowson, M. (2002). Performance approach, performance avoidance and depth of information processing: A fresh look at relations between students' academic motivation and cognition. *Educational Psychology: An International Journal of Experimental Educational Psychology*, *22*(5), 571–589.
Bastick, T. (2000). Why teacher trainees choose the teaching profession: Comparing trainees in metropolitan and developing countries. *International Review of Education*, *46*(3), 343–349.
Bielby, G., Sharp, C., Shuayb, M., Teeman, D., Keys, W., & Benefield, P. (2007). *Recruitment and retention on initial teacher training: A systematic review*. www.diversityinleadership.co.uk/index.php?p=20
Brookhart, S. M., & Freeman, D. J. (1992). Characteristics of entering teacher candidates. *Review of Educational Research*, *62*(1), 37.
Canrinus, E. T., & Fokkens-Bruinsma, M. (2014). Changes in student teachers' motives and the meaning of teacher education program quality. *European Journal of Teacher Education*, *37*(3), 262–278.
Cavanagh, S. (2007). Teaching viewed as stable and respectable profession. *Education Week*, *26*(41), 8–10.
Chan, K.-W. (2006). In-service teachers' motives and commitment in teaching. *Hong Kong Teachers' Centre Journal*, *5*, 112–128.
Cheng, M. M. H., Tang, S. Y. F., & Cheng, A. Y. N. (2015). Interpreting ambivalence regarding motivation for teaching among student-teachers. *Asia-Pacific Education Researcher*, *24*(1), 147–156.
Chivore, B. R. S. (1988). Factors determining the attractiveness of the teaching profession in Zimbabwe. *International Review of Education/Internationale Zeitschrift für Erziehungswissenschaft/Revue internationale de pédagogie*, *34*(1), 59–78.
Cochran-Smith, M., & Zeichner, K. M. (Eds.). (2005). *Studying teacher education: The report of the AERA panel on research and teacher education*. Lawrence Erlbaum Associates.
Corbin, J. M., & Strauss, A. L. (1990). *Basics of qualitative research: Grounded theory procedures and techniques*. Sage Publications.
Covington, M. V., & Müeller, K. J. (2001). Intrinsic versus extrinsic motivation: An approach/avoidance reformulation. *Educational Psychology Review*, *13*(2), 157–176.
Darling-Hammond, L., LaFors, J., & Snyder, J. (2001). Educating teachers for California's future. *Teacher Education Quarterly*, *28*(1), 9–55.
Deci, E. L., & Ryan, R. M. (2000). The "what" and "why" of goal pursuits: Human needs and the self-determination of behavior. *Psychological Inquiry*, *11*(4), 227–268.
Di, Y., Feng, S., & Tan, Y. (2022). Jiyu jiaoxue zhiliang de gongfei shifan jiaoyu zhengce yanjiu [Research on the policy-funded normal students' education from the perspective of teaching quality]. *Jiao Yu Ke Xue*, *38*(1), 49–56.
Doliopoulou, E. (1995). The motives for the selection of the teaching profession by future kindergarten teachers and the factors which form their later opinion of their profession. *International Journal of Early Childhood*, *27*(1), 28–35.
Dörnyei, Z. N., & Ushioda, E. (2011). *Teaching and researching motivation*. Longman.
Drudy, S., & Ebooks, C. (2005). *Men and the classroom: Gender imbalances in teaching*. Routledge.
Edmonds, S., Sharp, C., & Benefield, P. (2002). *Recruitment to and retention in initial teacher training: A systematic review*. http://195.194.2.34/htmldocs/Outcome_TSR.doc

Evans, H. (1993). The choice of teaching as a career. *Social and Economic Studies*, *42*(2/3), 225–242.
Fan, C.-T. (2010). Jiaqiang mianfei shifansheng qunti de sixiang zhengzhi jiaoyu tanxi [Ideological and political education for policy-funded pre-service teachers: Problems and suggestion]. *Xi Nan Nong Ye Da Xue Xue Bao (She Hui Ke Xue Ban)*, *8*(5), 257–259.
Feng, Z.-Q., Jiang, Y., Du, Y.-T., & Gao, Q. (2010). Mianfei shifansheng jiaoshi zhiye renting jiqi yingxiang yinsu yanjiu [Teaching professional identity of the students with free-tuition]. *He Bei Shi Fan Da Xue Xue Bao (Jiao Yu Ke Xue Ban)*, *12*(7), 69–75.
Ferrell, C. M., & Daniel, L. G. (1993). *Construct validation of an instrument measuring teacher career motivations*. Paper presented at the Annual Meeting of the Mid-South Educational Research Association, New Orleans, LA.
Fokkens-Bruinsma, M., & Canrinus, E. T. (2012). The factors influencing teaching (FIT)-choice scale in a Dutch teacher education program. *Asia-Pacific Journal of Teacher Education*, *40*(3), 249–269.
Fokkens-Bruinsma, M., & Canrinus, E. T. (2014). Motivation for becoming a teacher and engagement with the profession: Evidence from different contexts. *International Journal of Educational Research*, *65*, 65–74.
Gao, X.-S., & Trent, J. (2009). Understanding mainland Chinese students' motivations for choosing teacher education programmes in Hong Kong. *Journal of Education for Teaching*, *35*(2), 145–159.
Glaser, B. G., & Strauss, A. L. (1968). *The discovery of grounded theory: Strategies for qualitative research*. Weidenfeld and Nicolson.
Goh, K. C., & Atputhasamy, L. (2001). *Teacher education in Singapore: What motivates students to choose teaching as a career?* Paper presented at the International Educational Research Conference, University of Notre Dame, Fremantle, Western Australia.
Goodson, I., & Hargreaves, A. (1996). *Teachers' professional lives* (Vol. 3). Falmer Press.
Gordon, J. A. (2000). Asian American resistance to selecting teaching as a career: The power of community and tradition. *Teachers College Record*, *102*(1), 173–196.
Gu, M.-Y., & Lai, C. (2012). Motivation and commitment: Pre-service teachers from Hong Kong and Mainland China at a training institute in Hong Kong. *Teacher Education Quarterly*, *39*(3), 45.
Guarino, C. M., Santibanez, L., & Daley, G. A. (2006). Teacher recruitment and retention: A review of the recent empirical literature. *Review of Educational Research*, *76*(2), 173–208.
Hatch, J. A. (1999). What preservice teachers can learn from studies of teachers' work. *Teaching and Teacher Education*, *15*(3), 229–242.
Heinz, M. (2013). Why choose teaching in the Republic of Ireland? Student teachers' motivations and perceptions of teaching as a career and their evaluations of Irish second-level education. *European Journal of Educational Studies*, *5*(1), 1–17.
Ivan, R., & Jonathan, C. (1997). Why did secondary PGCE students choose teaching as a career? *Research in Education*, *58*, 46–58.
Joseph, P. B., & Green, N. (1986). Perspectives on reasons for becoming teachers. *Journal of Teacher Education*, *37*(6), 28–33.
Klassen, R. M., Al-Dhafri, S., Hannok, W., & Betts, S. M. (2011). Investigating pre-service teacher motivation across cultures using the teachers' ten statements test. *Teaching and Teacher Education*, *27*(3), 579–588.

Kobori, M., & Kyriacou, C. (1998). Motivation to learn and teach English in Slovenia. *Educational Studies*, *24*(3), 345–351.
König, J., & Rothland, M. (2012). Motivations for choosing teaching as a career: Effects on general pedagogical knowledge during initial teacher education. *Asia-Pacific Journal of Teacher Education*, *40*(3), 289–315.
Kyriacou, C., & Benmansour, N. (1999). Motivation to become a teacher of a foreign language. *The Language Learning Journal*, *19*(1), 69–72.
Kyriacou, C., & Coulthard, M. (2000). Undergraduates' views of teaching as a career choice. *Journal of Education for Teaching*, *26*(2), 117.
Kyriacou, C., Hultgren, Å., & Stephens, P. (1999). Student teachers' motivation to become a secondary school teacher in England and Norway. *Teacher Development*, *3*(3), 373–381.
Lai, K.-C., Chan, K.-W., Ko, K.-W., & So, K.-S. (2005). Teaching as a career: A perspective from Hong Kong senior secondary students. *Journal of Education for Teaching*, *31*(3), 153–168.
Lau, W. H. (1968). *Why teach? A study of motives for teaching as a career (Unpublished paper)*.
Li, G.-F. (2010). Mianfei shifansheng baokao dongji de diaocha yanjiu – yi Shaanxi shifan daxue weili [Survey research on university-entry motivations of policy-funded pre-service teachers – Shaanxi Normal University as an example]. *Hei Long Jiang Gao Jiao Yan Jiu*, *6*, 1–4.
Li, G.-F. (2011). Mianfei shifansheng baokao dongji de diaocha yu fenxi – yi Shaanxi shifan daxue weili [Investigating and analysing policy-funded pre-service teachers' motivations to enter teacher-training programmes – A case study from Shaanxi Normal University]. *Guo Jia Jiao Yu Xing Zheng Xue Yuan Xue Bao*, *161*(5), 71–74.
Li, L., Huang, Y.-Y., Xu, X.-C., & Han, Y.-M. (2013). The relationship between entry motivation and professional satisfaction of no-fee preservice students. *Chinese Education & Society*, *46*(2), 43–61.
Li, L., & Niyozov, S. (2008). Negotiating teachers professional identity in a changing Chinese society. *Education and Society*, *26*(2), 69–84.
Lin, E., Shi, Q.-M., Wang, J., Zhang, S.-A., & Liu, H. (2012). Initial motivations for teaching: Comparison between preservice teachers in the United States and China. *Asia-Pacific Journal of Teacher Education*, *40*(3), 227–248.
Liu, L.-L. (2009). *Mianfei shifansheng ruxue dongji, xuexi ziwo xiaonenggan he zhuanye chengnuo de xianzhuang jiqi guanxi yanjiu [A study on enrolment motivation, perceived academic self-efficacy and professional commitment of free teacher education students and their relationship]* [Unpublished Thesis for Master-Degree in Developmental and Educational Psychology, Southwest University].
Liu, P. (2010). Examining perspectives of entry-level teacher candidates: A comparative study. *Australian Journal of Teacher Education*, *35*(5), 56–78.
Liu, W., & Li, Q. (2022). Weihe congjiao: Gongfei shifansheng yu feigongfei shifansheng congjiao dongji de duozu qianleibie fenxi [Why teach: A multi-group latent class analysis of government-funded student teachers' and non-government-funded student teachers' motivation to teach]. *Zhong guo gao jiao yan jiu*, *10*, 61–67.
Liu, Y. (2009). Mianfei shifansheng shijiaoxia zhongxiaoxue jiaoshizhiye de youshi yu buzu [The advantages and disadvantages of teaching profession in primary and secondary schools: Views of the policy-funded pre-service teachers in China]. *Wang Luo Cai Fu Jiao Yu Qian Yan*, *3*, 15–16.

Lortie, D. C. (1975). *Schoolteacher: A sociological study*. The University of Chicago Press.

Losh, S., & Wilke, R. (2008). Beyond belief: Preservice teachers' planned instructional strategies. *Action in Teacher Education, 30*(3), 64.

Lovett, S. (2007). "Teachers of promise": Is teaching their first career choice? *New Zealand Annual Review of Education, 16*, 29–53.

Low, E. L., Lim, S. K., Ch'ng, A., & Goh, K. C. (2011). Pre-service teachers' reasons for choosing teaching as a career in Singapore. *Asia Pacific Journal of Education, 31*(2), 195–210.

Ma, Y., & Cui, S. (2017). Zhongguo mianfei shifansheng yanjiu shinian huigu yu qianzhan – – jiyu hexin qikan xiangguan wenxian de neirong fenxi [A review and prospect of recent ten years researches on free normal education of China: Content analysis based on core journal articles]. *Ke Cheng Jiao Cai Jiao Fa, 37*(8).

Moran, A., Kilpatrick, R., Abbott, L., Dallat, J., & McClune, B. (2001). Training to teach: Motivating factors and implications for recruitment. *Evaluation & Research in Education, 15*(1), 17–32.

Olaseboye Olasehinde, M. (1972). An analytical study of the motives of primary school teachers for choosing teaching as a career. *Journal of Teacher Education, 23*(2), 207–210.

Pan, D., & Wang, M. (2020). Cong gongfei shifansheng dao buxi jiangshi: Nanxing xueqian jiaoshi de zhiye xuanze yu shenfen rentong – jiyu xin ziyou zhuyi shijiao de gean pouxi [From government-paid teacher education students to tutors: The career choice and identity of male pre-school education teachers – a case study based on neoliberalism]. *Xue Qian Jiao Yu Yan Jiu, 303*(3), 31–41.

Papanastasiou, C., & Papanastasiou, E. (1997). Factors that influence students to become teachers. *Educational Research and Evaluation: An International Journal on Theory and Practice, 3*(4), 305–316.

Richardson, P. W., & Watt, H. M. G. (2005). "I've decided to become a teacher": Influences on career change. *Teaching and Teacher Education, 21*(5), 475–489.

Richardson, P. W., & Watt, H. M. G. (2006). Who chooses teaching and why? Profiling characteristics and motivations across three Australian universities. *Asia-Pacific Journal of Teacher Education, 34*(1), 27–56.

Richardson, P. W., & Watt, H. M. G. (2010). Current and future directions in teacher motivation research. In T. C. Urdan & S. A. Karabenick (Eds.), *The decade ahead: Applications and contexts of motivation and achievement (Advances in motivation and achievement, Vol. 16)* (pp. 139–173). Emerald Group Publishing Limited.

Roberson, S. D., Keith, T. Z., & Page, E. B. (1983). Now who aspires to teach? *Educational Researcher, 12*(6), 13–21.

Roness, D. (2011). Still motivated? The motivation for teaching during the second year in the profession. *Teaching and Teacher Education, 27*(3), 628–638.

Rury, J. L. (1986). Gender, salaries, and career: American teachers, 1900–1910. *Issues in Education, 4*(3), 215.

Saban, A. (2003). A Turkish profile of prospective elementary school teachers and their views of teaching. *Teaching and Teacher Education, 19*(8), 829–846.

Shak, J. (2022). Motivations for entering into a teaching career in Brunei Darussalam: An update. *Teaching and Teacher Education, 117*.

Sinclair, C. (2008). Initial and changing student teacher motivation and commitment to teaching. *Asia-Pacific Journal of Teacher Education, 36*(2), 79–104.

Sinclair, C., Dowson, M., & McInerney, D. M. (2006). Motivations to teach: Psychometric perspectives across the first semester of teacher education. *Teachers College Record*, *108*(6), 1132–1154.

Soh, K. C. (1989). *Motives for teaching of female certificate in education students (Research paper ERU/9/89)* (9789971953652, 997195365X). http://canterbury.summon.serialssolutions.com/2.0.0/link/0/eLvHCXMwY2BQAM3YJqUZJZkkJpkmJlomWiSZJlukJaWlWholASuIZJQdrkiluZsQA1NqniiDjJtriLOHLmjCIr4AcuZ-CvKsLaCTa3MBQjIE3EbT2O68EvEcsRYJBwTjFyNQIaA0od5ukppgmmiSnpBkaAVMeMAUnpqYCAHDlJY4

Su, J. Z. X. (1993). The study of the education of educators: A profile of teacher education students. *Journal of Research and Development in Education*, *26*(3), 125–132.

Su, Z.-X., Hawkins, J. N., Huang, T., & Zhao, Z.-Y. (2001). Choices and commitment: A comparison of teacher candidates' profiles and perspectives in China and the United States. *International Review of Education*, *47*(6), 611–635.

Summerhill, A., Matranga, M., Peltier, G., & Hill, G. (1998). High school seniors' perceptions of a teaching career. *Journal of Teacher Education*, *49*(3), 228–234.

Sun, M.-T., & Chu, X. (2008). Shifansheng mianfei jiaoyu zhengce de xianzhuang ji fansi [Reviewing and reflecting on studies of government-funded teacher education policy]. *Dang Dai Jiao Yu Lun Tan (Xiao Zhang Jiao Yu Yan Jiu)*, *18*(6), 12–16.

Sun, Z.-H. (2011). Jin wunian lai zhongguo jiaoyu zhengce yanjiu redian zongshu [An overview of research interests on Chinese educational policies in recent five years]. *Shi Ji Qiao*, *232*(17), 123–125.

Suryani, A. (2021). "I chose teacher education because . . .": A look into Indonesian future teachers. *Asia Pacific Journal of Education*, *41*(1), 70–88.

Tang, S. Y. F., Cheng, M. M. H., & Cheng, A. Y. N. (2014). Shifts in teaching motivation and sense of self-as-teacher in initial teacher education. *Educational Review*, *66*(4), 465–481.

Tang, S. Y. F., Wong, A. K. Y., & Cheng, M. M. H. (2015). The preparation of highly motivated and professionally competent teachers in initial teacher education. *Journal of Education for Teaching*, *41*(2), 128–144.

Tang, S. Y. F., Wong, P. M., Wong, A. K. Y., & Cheng, M. M. H. (2018). What attracts young people to become teachers? A comparative study of pre-service student teachers' motivation to become teachers in Hong Kong and Macau. *Asia Pacific Education Review*, *19*(3), 433–444.

Thomson, M. M., Turner, J. E., & Nietfeld, J. L. (2012). A typological approach to investigate the teaching career decision: Motivations and beliefs about teaching of prospective teacher candidates. *Teaching and Teacher Education*, *28*(3), 324–335.

Topkaya, E. Z., & Uztosun, M. S. (2012). Choosing teaching as a career: Motivations of pre-service English teachers in Turkey. *Journal of Language Teaching and Research*, *3*(1), 126–134.

Wang, H. H., & Fwu, B. J. (2001). Why teach? The motivation and commitment of graduate students of a teacher education program in a research university. *Proceedings of the National Science Council*, *11*(4), 390–400.

Wang, T.-Z., Xu, Q., Li, H.-W., & Li, L.-Z. (2013). Woguo shifansheng mianfei jiaoyu yanjiu redian de lingyu goucheng yu tuozhan qushi – jiyu CNKI xueshu qikan 2007–2012 nian wenxian de gongci keshihua fenxi [Domains and trends of studies on the government-funded teacher education policy in China – A co-word and data visualisation analysis on publications from 2007 to 2012 in CNKI]. *Jiao Yu Yan Jiu, 407*(12), 102–109.

Wang, X., & Niu, X. (2023). Fuquan lilun shijiao xia gongfei shifansheng dui jiaoshi zhiye de renzhi yu xuanze [Government-funded normal university students' cognition and choice of the teaching profession from the perspective of empowerment theory]. *Jiao Shi Jiao Yu Xue Bao, 1*, 59–68.

Wang, Z.-C. (2011). Shifansheng mianfei jiaoyu zhengce shishi xianzhuang diaocha ji sikao [Investigation and reflection on the implementation of the Central Government-Funded Teacher Education Policy]. *Xian Dai Jiao Yu Guan Li, 1*.

Williams, J., & Forgasz, H. (2009). The motivations of career change students in teacher education. *Asia-Pacific Journal of Teacher Education, 37*(1), 95–108.

Wu, Q., Lin, Y., & Gong, H. (2022). Weihe xuanze shifan jiaoyu zhuanye? Jiyu xianyu gaozhong biyesheng daxue zhuanye xuanze de shizheng yanjiu [Why choose a major in education: An empirical study based on the college major choices of county high school graduates]. *Zhong Guo Gao Jiao Yan Jiu, 12*, 51–58.

Yao, Y., & Dong, X.-W. (2009). Quanguo shifansheng mianfei jiaoyu zhengce shishi rentongdu diaocha [Investigating the degree of recognition on implementing the government-funded teacher education policy in China]. *Jiao Yu Yan Jiu Yu Shi Yan, 126*(1), 45–50.

Yao, Y., Ma, L., & Li, X.-H. (2012). Shifansheng mianfei zhengce shishi xiaoguo de yanjiu – jiyu shoujie mianfei shifansheng de ruxue yu biye diaocha [A study on implementations of the tuition-free policy for student teacher]. *Jiao Shi Jiao Yu Yan Jiu, 24*(2), 63–68.

Ye, W. B., Ding, Y. Y., Han, X. M., & Ye, W. Q. (2022). Pre-service teachers' teaching motivation and perceptions of teacher morality in China. *Educational Studies*. DOI: 10.1080/03055698.2022.2037406

Yong, B. C. S. (1995). Teacher trainees' motives for entering into a teaching career in Brunei Darussalam. *Teaching and Teacher Education, 11*(3), 275–280.

Younger, M., Brindley, S., Pedder, D., & Hagger, H. (2004). Starting points: Student teachers' reasons for becoming teachers and their preconceptions of what this will mean. *European Journal of Teacher Education, 27*(3), 245–264.

Yu, S. L. (2015). Becoming a teacher in a gambling city: A case study of two pre-service teachers' motivation for teaching in Macau. *Journal of Education for Teaching, 41*(4), 447–450.

Zhang, X.-H., & Zhao, H.-H. (2016). Zhengce manyidu, jiaoshi zhichi dui mianfei shifansheng zhiye rentong de zuoyong: Congjiao dongji de zhongjie xiaoying [The roles of educational policy satisfaction and faculty support on pre-service teachers' professional identity: The mediating effect of teaching motivation]. *Xin Li Fa Zhan Yu Jiao Yu, 32*(6), 725–732.

Zhao, H. (2008). Why did people become secondary-school English as a foreign language teachers in China? An examination of the pathways, motivations and policy through a life-history narrative approach. *Educational Research for Policy and Practice, 7*(3), 183–195.

Zhao, H.-Y., Qi, T.-T., Zhang, X.-H., & Lvqiu, Y.-C. (2011). Mianfei shifansheng de jiaoshi zhiye renting: Jiegou yu tedian shizheng yanjiu [Teacher professional identity of tuition-free normal college students: Structure and character]. *Jiao Shi Jiao Yu Yan Jiu, 23*(6), 62–66.

Zhao, P. (2012). Mianfei shifansheng zhengce yanjiu de fangfalun pingshu [Review on research methodologies in free teacher education policy studies]. *Jiao Shi Jiao Yu Yan Jiu, 24*(3), 41–48.

Zhou, Q. (2013). Mianfei shifansheng zhengce renzhi diaocha – yi xinan daxue wei gean [Investigation on the free normal students' cognitive of policy: Take Southwest University as a case]. *Jiao Shi Jiao Yu Yan Jiu, 25*(3), 60–65.

3 Mixed-Methods Research Design

Introduction

This study employs a mixed-methods research design to comprehensively explore the impacts of the CGFTE policy. The quantitative approaches form the foundation for statistically and comparatively analysing the impacts of the funding policy, and the qualitative study serves as an add-on to further interpret the quantitative results. The research instruments employed in this study include Part B of the FIT-Choice scale and a self-developed interview outline. A pilot study was conducted to ensure the validity and reliability of these research tools. Additionally, this chapter delineates ethical considerations that ensured the protection of participants' rights and welfare, outlines the criteria for participant recruitment, and describes the quantitative and qualitative data collection processes.

3.1 Research Design Overview

The CGFTE policy has been implemented in the top six national teacher-training universities under the Ministry of Education in the People's Republic of China since 2007. Many other teacher-training universities and colleges do not have similar funding policies. This makes it possible to compare students from the two groups of universities. By examining the differences in teaching career-choice motivation between PFPTs and their self-sponsored counterparts, it will be possible to infer the impacts of this policy. Based on previous studies that recommended using both quantitative and qualitative methods to investigate teaching motivation in order to gain more meaningful insights and understand the uniqueness of certain types of career-choice motivation (Wong et al., 2014), this study employed a mixed-methods research design.

The quantitative design consisted of three main stages. First, the survey questionnaire on career-choice motivation was adapted and revised following a pilot study. Then, the questionnaire was administered to over 700 Chinese pre-service teachers from three teacher-training universities in 2013, one that implemented the CGFTE policy and two that did not. Finally, the data collected from the two groups of teacher training universities were compared in terms of teaching career choice motivation, with a focus on identifying statistically significant differences between the two groups to determine the potential impacts of the CGFTE policy on Chinese pre-service teachers.

The qualitative design served as a complementary approach to the quantitative study. Building on the quantitative findings, an interview outline was developed, and participants were selected. In both 2014 and 2022, online in-depth interviews were conducted with ten PFPTs whose satisfaction levels with the CGFTE policy varied. Narrative stories about their personal experiences were then compiled to explore the complexity and richness of their motivations for choosing teaching as a future career, adding another layer to the quantitative findings.

3.2 Research Tools

3.2.1 Part B of the FIT-Choice Scale

The survey questionnaire used in the present study was self-reported and contained two major sections. The first section (refer to Appendix 1) asked participants to report their demographic information, such as gender, ethnicity, and hometown. The second section was the main body, which comprised a Likert-type (1 to 7) self-reported scale – Part B of the Factors Influencing Teaching Choice scale (FIT-Choice Scale) developed by Richardson and Watt (2006). Part B of the FIT-Choice scale, also named the Career-Choice Motivation scale (CCM Scale, refer to Appendix 2) in this study, consisted of 38 items. It was empirically validated in the Australian context where the scale demonstrated "sound convergent and divergent construct validity and good reliability" (Watt & Richardson, 2007, p. 195). Subsequently, it was applied in many Western contexts (e.g., Kilinc et al., 2012; Lin et al., 2012; Richardson & Watt, 2006; Watt & Richardson, 2008; Watt et al., 2012).

At the beginning of the scale, an introduction was provided about the purpose of the scale and the specific meaning of each number in the Likert scale that needed to be selected to complete the survey. The entire questionnaire concluded with an invitation for participants to take part in further interviews, and contact information was requested to be left if participants agreed to be involved.

3.2.2 Semi-Structured Interview Outline

To explore the complexity and richness of different PFPTs' motivations for choosing a teaching career, as well as their perceptions towards the CGFTE policy, a semi-structured interview outline was developed. The outline (refer to Appendix 3) consisted of five questions and some sub-questions in three categories: (1) background information, such as major and personal interests; (2) reasons for choosing a teaching career; and (3) comments on the CGFTE policy, particularly on the restrictive policy terms. The sub-questions were used to expand and deepen the participants' responses, and the researcher also asked impromptu questions beyond the outline when necessary.

3.3 Pilot Study

To test the appropriateness of the Chinese translations for the survey questionnaire and its effectiveness in the Chinese context, an online pilot study was conducted. The initial Chinese version of the questionnaire was posted online using SurveyMonkey software, which included comment boxes for feedback on the explicitness and suitability of the questionnaire items. Subsequently, an invitation email was sent to nine Chinese native speakers, stating the purpose of the pilot study and attaching the links to the online survey. Feedback and suggestions from participants in the comment boxes were analysed, and adjustments were made to the initial questionnaire, including changing some Chinese translations of Part B of the FIT-Choice scale (refer to Appendix 4). Some participants suggested that the demographic section did not cover enough information about the participants. After consulting the literature reviewed in this study, more demographic information, namely, ethnicity, family income, National College Entrance Examination (NCEE) scores, school level, and school subject (refer to Appendix 1), was added to the study instrument.

In addition, a minor pilot study was conducted to test the effectiveness of the interview outline (refer to Appendix 3) designed for this study. Four PhD students majoring in education, two native Chinese speakers and two native English speakers, were invited to participate in the pilot study. Each of them was interviewed face-to-face by the researcher for around one hour in a research office. During the interviews, the researcher noted any problems with the self-designed interview outline. At the end of each interview, the interviewee was asked for suggestions to improve the interview outline. Minor changes were made to the wording of some questions in the outline accordingly.

3.4 Ethical Considerations

Protecting the rights of participants is of utmost importance. Prior to data collection, ethical approval was granted, and permission to use the FIT-Choice scale and its Chinese translation in the present study was obtained. During quantitative data collection, the leaders of the three targeted universities, course lecturers, and pre-service teachers received a letter (information sheet and consent form) introducing the study and requesting their voluntary participation, and during the qualitative data collection, all interviewees received the same letter. Participants who agreed to participate were recruited.

The participants' contact information provided in the questionnaires was solely used for follow-up studies. The researcher ensured that the interviews were conducted in a respectful and understanding manner. When creating narrative stories in the qualitative study, pseudonyms were used to protect their identities. All data collected in this study were treated confidentially.

3.5 Collection of Quantitative Data

The quantitative data were collected in 2013 from three targeted teacher-training universities: University A, University B, and University C. These data are still relevant as the CGFTE policy has been basically unchanged over the past decade. These three universities were located in the less developed southwest or centre of China, and the pre-service teachers sampled from them came from all over the country. University A implemented the CGFTE policy, and Universities B and C did not. The researcher for this study selected University A from the six universities carrying out the CGFTE policy for several reasons. Firstly, University A enrolled high school graduates from provinces all over China as pre-service teachers, making it an appropriate choice for a nationwide sample. Secondly, it had the largest number of pre-service teachers among the six policy universities (Li, 2011; Wei, 2007). Lastly, University A's national university ranking was in the middle among the six policy universities (Chinese University Alumni Association, 2014), indicating that its participants could offer a reasonably representative sample of PFPTs in China.

Information sheets and consent forms requesting permission to access the universities for the study were sent. After receiving signed consent forms, the researcher entered University A in Chongqing Municipality and collected data for one month in May 2013. In June 2013, the researcher travelled to Hunan Province and collected data from University B for another month. Because of time constraints, a staff member at University C in Sichuan Province assisted the researcher in collecting data for one month in June 2013.

Upon arriving at each university campus, the researcher consulted the university curriculum schedule and randomly selected ten classrooms where first-year or last-year pre-service teachers from different colleges were taking courses. Before entering a classroom, the researcher presented the course lecturer with the information sheet and the consent form and obtained their signed consent to conduct the survey. Based on the principle of voluntary participation, the researcher then distributed the questionnaires, along with the information sheet and consent form, to the pre-service teachers in the classroom. After approximately 25 minutes, the pre-service teachers who volunteered to participate completed the questionnaires, which were then returned to the researcher.

A total of 782 questionnaires were distributed among pre-service teachers in the three universities, and 717 were returned. Of those returned, 328 included contact information indicating agreement to participate further.

44 Mixed-Methods Research Design

These participants were from different colleges at each university and were studying various majors, which meant they would be teaching diverse subjects in primary or secondary schools after graduation. As five returned questionnaires had one or more incomplete sections and were excluded, the final number of valid respondents for the survey was 712. Therefore, the data collection had a response rate of 91.7%. All data from the 712 gathered questionnaires were entered into SPSS 22.0 files for quantitative data analysis.

3.6 Collection of Qualitative Data

Qualitative data were collected through online audio interviews with seven PFPTs in 2014 and three in 2022. The data collection process in 2014 involved several steps. Firstly, the researcher obtained the contact information of pre-service teachers who wished to participate in online interviews. After completing the questionnaire survey, participants were asked to leave their contact information for online interviews if they agreed to participate, and 328 pre-service teachers left their contact information. However, 156 self-sponsored pre-service teachers from the two non-policy universities (65 from University B and 91 from University C) were discarded because the targeted population in the qualitative study was PFPTs. Additionally, the 62 last-year PFPTs from University A were excluded as they were no longer pre-service teachers when the online interviews began. Therefore, the potential interview participants were the 110 first-year PFPTs from University A who left their contact information. After excluding three questionnaires with incomplete sections, the final pool for sampling online interviewees for this study was 107 first-year PFPTs (they were in the second year of study when participating in the interview).

Secondly, the researcher established a guideline for recruiting interviewees with different attitudes towards the CGFTE policy. Based on the results of the quantitative data analysis, the PFPTs were divided into three groups according to their satisfaction levels with the CGFTE policy: high, medium, and low. The distribution of the 107 participants with contact information among the three groups provided a guideline for sampling PFPTs with different attitudes towards the CGFTE policy.

Thirdly, because of time and financial limitations, the researcher planned to interview 12 PFPTs from the sample pool. Therefore, four PFPTs from each of the three groups were randomly selected using SPSS 22.0, and information sheets and consent forms were sent to them online through the contact details they provided. Seven invitees, three from the high satisfaction group, two from the medium satisfaction group, and two from the low satisfaction group, returned the signed consent forms online, indicating their agreement to participate in the online audio interview.

Finally, the online audio interviews with the seven PFPTs in China were conducted from January to February 2014 through the instant communication software QQ, which is widely used in China. To keep the study up to date, three more PFPTs at the same university with different attitudes towards the CGFTE policy were interviewed online in 2022. At the beginning of each interview, the researcher restated the purposes of the study, the required time duration, and the ethical considerations to the interviewee. During the interview, main questions on the interview outline (refer to Appendix 3) were asked. Sub-questions and follow-up questions were raised as needed to either clarify a response or elicit other relevant topics. All the interviews were conducted in Mandarin and recorded with the participants' approval. Each interview lasted for approximately one hour, and once completed, the audio recording was transcribed into a Word document in Chinese, which was then sent to the interviewee to read. After being approved by the interviewees, these Chinese transcripts were analysed, and narrative stories were created and presented in English. Following the quantitative data analysis, these narrative stories were expected to further demonstrate the "complexity and multiplicities" (Chase, 2011, p. 429) of the career-choice motivations of PFPTs whose attitudes towards the CGFTE policy were different.

References

Chase, S. E. (2011). Narrative inquiry: Still a field in the making. In N. K. Denzin & Y. S. Lincoln (Eds.), *The SAGE handbook of qualitative research* (4th ed.). SAGE Publications Ltd.

Chinese University Alumni Association. (2014). *Ranking list of the top 100 universities in China*. www.cuaa.net/cur/2014/

Kilinc, A., Watt, H. M. G., & Richardson, P. W. (2012). Factors influencing teaching choice in Turkey. *Asia-Pacific Journal of Teacher Education, 40*(3), 199–226.

Li, D.-X. (2011). *Southwest University newly developed 3 majors and 5 directions and recruited approximately 3000 policy-funded pre-service teachers*. http://edu.sina.com.cn/gaokao/2011-05-23/1616296695.shtml

Lin, E., Shi, Q.-M., Wang, J., Zhang, S.-A., & Liu, H. (2012). Initial motivations for teaching: Comparison between preservice teachers in the United States and China. *Asia-Pacific Journal of Teacher Education, 40*(3), 227–248.

Richardson, P. W., & Watt, H. M. G. (2006). Who chooses teaching and why? Profiling characteristics and motivations across three Australian universities. *Asia-Pacific Journal of Teacher Education, 34*(1), 27–56.

Watt, H. M. G., & Richardson, P. W. (2007). Motivational factors influencing teaching as a career choice: Development and validation of the FIT-choice scale. *The Journal of Experimental Education, 75*(3), 167–202.

Watt, H. M. G., & Richardson, P. W. (2008). Motivations, perceptions, and aspirations concerning teaching as a career for different types of beginning teachers. *Learning and Instruction, 18*(5), 408–428.

Watt, H. M. G., Richardson, P. W., Klusmann, U., Kunter, M., Beyer, B., Trautwein, U., & Baumert, J. (2012). Motivations for choosing teaching as a career: An international comparison using the FIT-choice scale. *Teaching and Teacher Education, 28*(6), 791–805.

Wei, L. (2007). Southwest University plans to recruit 2900 policy-funded pre-service teachers. *Gansu Daily*. http://exam.gansudaily.com.cn/system/2007/04/12/010319526.shtml

Wong, A. K. Y., Tang, S. Y. F., & Cheng, M. M. H. (2014). Teaching motivations in Hong Kong: Who will choose teaching as a fallback career in a stringent job market? *Teaching and Teacher Education, 41*, 81–91.

4 Quantitative Analysis of Data From 712 Chinese Pre-service Teachers and Results

Introduction

This chapter analyses the responses of 712 Chinese pre-service teachers to the two quantitative questions raised in the present study. After handling the missing values and presenting the demographic information of all participants, the data were loaded into SPSS 22.0 files and processed through various quantitative methods, including exploratory factor (principal component) analysis, independent-samples t test, and two-way between-group ANOVA. The results revealed that the six major motivations for Chinese pre-service teachers to choose teaching as a future career, in decreasing order of importance, were teacher influence, job advantages (extrinsic motivation), social value (altruistic motivation), personal interest (intrinsic motivation), others' suggestions, and fallback career. Among the motivation types, the pre-service teachers supported by the CGFTE policy rated "intrinsic motivation" significantly higher than the self-sponsored pre-service teachers, suggesting that the CGFTE policy attracts students with higher intrinsic career-choice motivation to the teacher-training programs. However, further analyses found that during the four-year teacher training, those funded by the policy experienced a decline in their intrinsic motivation to choose teaching as a profession, which is opposite to the trend for their self-sponsored counterparts. This indicates that the CGFTE policy may fail to increase or maintain Chinese pre-service teachers' intrinsic motivation to choose teaching as their future profession.

4.1 Handling Missing Data

The present study's quantitative data had a low level of missing values overall. The missing data for participants' background information were all lower than 10%, except for family monthly income, which had around 16.4% missing data. Participants' responses to the questionnaire items had even lower missing data, ranging from 0.56% for B1 to 2.11% for B37. After the following procedures, the present study's missing data were remedied, and the full quantitative data from 712 Chinese pre-service teachers were ready for analysis.

DOI: 10.4324/9781032639680-4

For the nonmetric variables of gender, nationality, and home region, the very small amount of missing data was checked individually and imputed based on clues such as the participant's existing information, the previous and next participants' information, and the majority's response to the same variable. The missing data in the nonmetric variables of school to teach and subject to teach were inferred and replaced based on records of the teacher-training programs the participants were enrolled in because they were usually consistent with the teacher-education programs.

For the metric variables, all the missing data were treated with expectation maximisation (EM) before the data analysis. The EM approach is effective, especially in situations when the missing values are non-random. In the present study, the relatively high rate of missing data in family monthly income (16.4%) could have been attributable to participants' reluctance to report it, but EM was a suitable imputation method for dealing with all the missing data in the metric variables. EM is a model-based method that consists of repeated stages of E and M. The E stage estimates the best possible value to replace the missing data, and then the M stage estimates parameters, such as means, standard deviations, and correlations, presuming the missing data were replaced. This process keeps going through the two stages and replaces the missing data when the change in the estimated values is inappreciable.

4.2 Demographic Information of Participants

The present study's participants consist of two groups of pre-service teachers: policy-funded pre-service teachers (PFPTs) and self-sponsored pre-service teachers (SSPTs). For both groups, participants' demographic information consisted of personal information (gender, ethnicity, and age), family background (home region, family income, and home division), and university profile (type of university, year of study, discipline category, NCEE score, school level to teach, and school subject to teach). The following sections describe and compare the demographic distribution of participants in the two groups.

4.2.1 Personal Information

Descriptive statistics analysis showed that the percentage of female pre-service teachers (67.8%) was approximately double that of their male counterparts (32.2%). This trend was similar in both the PFPT group (68.6% vs. 31.4%) and the SSPT group (67.2% vs. 32.8%), and the proportions of female and male pre-service teachers in the PFPT group did not significantly differ from those in the SSPT group ($\chi2 = .278$, $df = 1$, $p > .05$).

There were significantly more Han pre-service teachers (84.6%) than minority pre-service teachers (15.4%). This was true in both the PFPT group and the SSPT group. However, the PFPT group had 14.4% more minority pre-service teachers than the SSPT group. According to the results of the chi-square test ($\chi 2 = 76.965$, df = 1, p < .001), the proportions of Han and minority pre-service teachers in the PFPT group (76.4% vs. 23.6%) significantly differed from those in the SSPT group (90.8% vs. 9.2%). Overall, most pre-service teachers (90%) were between the ages of 19 and 24. Half of them were between the ages of 19 and 21, and 40% were between the ages of 22 and 24. Only 10% of them were under 19 or over 24. Additionally, further analyses found that 90.9% of the pre-service teachers aged 21 or younger were in their first year of university study, and 98.2% of the pre-service teachers aged 22 or older were in their last year of university studies. Results from comparing pre-service teachers' year of study were very similar to those from comparing their age span. To avoid repetition, age span was not included in the following comparative analyses.

4.2.2 Family Background

Data analysis showed that the majority of pre-service teachers' homes were located in rural areas (69%), and only 31% of them came from urban areas. This trend was similar in both the PFPT group and the SSPT group. However, the SSPT group had a higher percentage (74.9%) of pre-service teachers from rural areas than the PFPT group (61.2%), and this difference was statistically significant ($\chi 2 = 31.007$, df = 1, p < .001).

Overall, almost half (46.1%) of pre-service teachers reported their monthly family income as no more than 2,000 RMB, about one third (29.5%) reported it as 2,001 to 4,000 RMB, and a quarter (24.4%) reported it as over 4,000 RMB.[1] However, this distribution was not mirrored in the two groups. In the PFPT group, an almost equal number of pre-service teachers ($\chi 2 = .058$, df = 2, p > .05) reported their monthly family income as no more than 2,000 RMB (32.7%), 2,001 to 4,000 RMB (33.7%), and over 4,000 RMB (33.7%). In the SSPT group, over half (56.3%) of pre-service teachers reported that their monthly family income was below 2,000 RMB, around a quarter (26.3%) reported it as between 2,000 and 4,000 RMB, and only 17.4% reported it as over 4,000 RMB. According to the results of the chi-square test, the number of PFPTs in the three income brackets significantly differed from that of the SSPTs ($\chi 2 = 83.898$, df = 2, p < .001).

As shown in Figure 4.1, the 712 pre-service teachers in this study came from over 30 regions in China. The first three regions where most of the pre-service teachers' homes were located were Sichuan Province (36.4%), Hunan Province (15.7%), and Chongqing Municipality (6.2%). All three regions are located in the southwest and middle parts of China, where the economy is less developed than the east and coastal areas of the country.

4.2.3 University Profile

In this study, 43.4%, 25.7%, and 30.9% of pre-service teachers were from University A, University B, and University C, respectively. All pre-service

50 Quantitative Analysis of Chinese Pre-service Teachers' Data

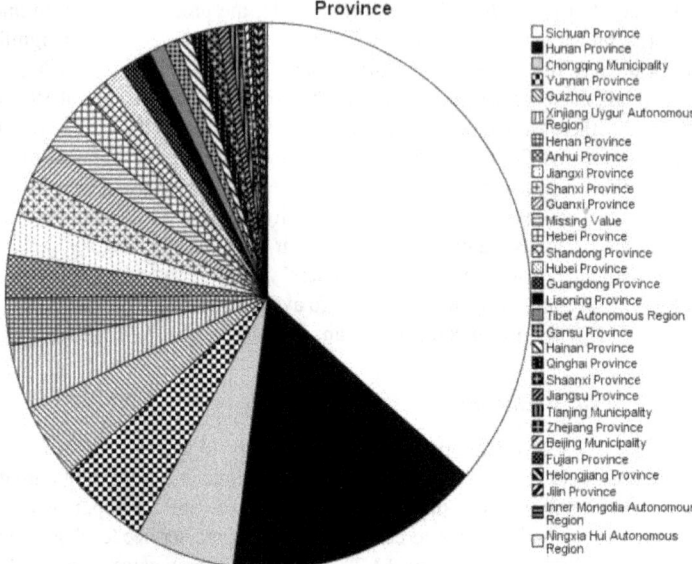

Figure 4.1 Province Distribution of the 712 Participants' Homes

teachers from University A were fully funded by the government (PFPTs), while those from the other two universities were self-sponsored (SSPTs).

There were no significant differences between the numbers of first-year and last-year pre-service teachers in this study (54.2% vs. 45.8%). This trend was similar in both the PFPT group and the SSPT group (PFPT group: $\chi2 = .935$, $df = 1$, $p > .05$). Moreover, the proportions of first-year and last-year pre-service teachers in the PFPT group did not significantly differ from those in the SSPT group ($\chi2 = .812$, $df = 1$, $p > .05$). Additionally, further analyses found that most (82.3%) of first-year pre-service teachers were between the ages of 19 and 21, and the majority (85.8%) of last-year pre-service teachers were between 21 and 24 years old.

The overwhelming majority of pre-service teachers (99%) were majoring in either liberal arts (55.2%) or science (43.8%). Only a few (1%) were in mixed subjects. For further analyses, the only PFPT with mixed subjects was placed in the liberal arts category. For the six SSPTs with mixed subjects, half were placed in the liberal arts category, and the other half were placed in the science category. There were 28.5% more liberal arts pre-service teachers than science teachers in the PFPT group ($\chi2 = 25.634$, $df = 1$, $p < .001$), whereas in the SSPT group, the numbers of pre-service teachers in the two study areas were almost equal ($\chi2 = .122$, $df = 1$, $p > .05$).

About half (51.8%) of pre-service teachers reported that their NCEE scores surpassed the bar set by their university by 24 points or less (these students were labelled the low score group). Approximately 40% of them reported their scores were 25 to 50 points higher than the bar (labelled the medium score group), and about 9% exceeded it by over 50 points (labelled the high score group). A similar trend existed in both the PFPT group and the SSPT group. However, in the PFPT group, there were 13% more pre-service teachers in the high score group than in the SSPT group ($\chi2 = 182.599$, df = 2, p < .001).

After graduation, nearly three-quarters (74.3%) of pre-service teachers planned to become junior or senior high school teachers. Approximately 15% of them wanted to teach in other educational institutions, and slightly over 10% had not yet decided. This trend was partially echoed in the two groups. In the PFPT group, more than 60% of pre-service teachers planned to become senior high school teachers, and only about 14% planned to teach in junior high schools. In the SSPT group, however, there were approximately 20% fewer pre-service teachers who planned to teach in senior high schools and about 10% more who wanted to teach in junior high schools than in the PFPT group. As for those who had not decided which school level to teach, only 0.6% of the PFPTs were undecided, in contrast with 17.6% of the SSPTs.

The pre-service teachers were going to teach more than ten school subjects. Overall, 44.3% of pre-service teachers reported that they were going to teach English (20.6%), math (14%), or Chinese (9.7%). Eight percent of participants had not decided yet. More PFPTs reported that they would teach politics (16.2%) and chemistry (11%), but more SSPTs reported that they would teach geography (10.7%) and physics (8.7%). There was a significant gap between the percentages of pre-service teachers who had not yet decided which subject to teach in the PFPT group (1%) and the SSPT group (14.1%).

To summarise, this quantitative study sampled 712 Chinese pre-service teachers in 2013 from three universities in China. Approximately half of the participants were first-year undergraduates, and the other half were last-year undergraduates. Of the participants, 43% were PFPTs, and the others were self-sponsored. Over half of the participants were majoring in liberal arts, and the remainder were in science. All participants had passed the NCEE before attending teacher-training universities, and most were trained to teach a variety of subjects in middle and secondary schools.

Among the participants, the number of female pre-service teachers was approximately double that of their male counterparts, and the majority of them were Han Chinese. These pre-service teachers were generally young, ranging in age from 19 to 24. The geographical distribution of their home regions covered most regions of China; however, over half of them came from the less developed southwest and central parts of China. Additionally, most of these pre-service teachers came from rural-area families with relatively low family incomes.

Several demographic differences were found between the PFPTs and the SSPTs in this study. The population of policy-funded ethnic minority pre-service teachers was larger than that of self-sponsored minority pre-service teachers. More self-sponsored participants came from rural areas than those funded by the government, and those funded by the government appeared to have higher family incomes than their self-sponsored counterparts. Policy-funded participants generally had higher scores on the NCEE than their self-sponsored counterparts. Lastly, PFPTs were more determined to become a teacher than the SSPTs.

4.3 Career-Choice Motivation of Chinese Pre-service Teachers: Types and Importance

The first quantitative research question contained two sub-questions: What are the career-choice motivations of Chinese pre-service teachers, and what importance do they place on each motivation? To analyse the quantitative data for this research question, exploratory factor analysis with principal component analysis (PCA) was chosen as the major statistical technique, and both orthogonal and oblimin rotations were attempted to obtain the most appropriate factors.

4.3.1 Examining Assumptions in Factor Analysis

The instrument used to gather quantitative data was the Chinese version of the Career-Choice Motivation scale (CCM scale), which was Part B of the FIT-Choice scale (refer to Appendix 2). The CCM scale consisted of 38 variables (items). Data were gathered from 712 pre-service teachers, including both PFPTs and SSPTs. Therefore, there was an 18:1 ratio of cases to variables, which fell within the acceptable range for factor analysis (Hair et al., 2010). Moreover, the sample size of 712 provided an adequate basis for calculating correlations between the variables.

To further assess the appropriateness of factor analysis for the CCM scale, the researcher calculated the correlations, the measures of sampling adequacy (MSA), and the anti-image correlations among the full set of 38 variables. Firstly, examining the correlation matrix revealed that 599 of the 676 correlations (88.6%) were significant at the .01 level. The number of significant correlations at .01 for each item ranged from 12 (B10, B35) to 37 (B3, B8, B19, B21, and B34). Secondly, Bartlett's test of sphericity results indicated that the overall correlations were significant at .001. Moreover, the overall MSA was .936, and the MSA for each variable ranged from .702 (B27) to .970 (B20), all of which exceeded the "middling" value (.70 or above) according to the guidelines suggested by researchers (Kaiser, 1970, 1974; Kaiser & Rice, 1974). This indicates that the set of variables met the fundamental requirements for factor analysis. Finally, a visual inspection of the anti-image correlation values (the negative values of the partial correlations) found that only one value was greater than .50 (B15–B25), which again indicated the strength of interrelationships among the set of variables. To summarise, all these measures demonstrated that the set of variables was appropriate for factor analysis.

4.3.2 Principal Component Analysis and Results

Principal component analysis was conducted to examine if the variables on the CCM scale could be reduced and grouped into identifiable clusters of variables, which in turn were the major career-choice motivations. Variables with no significant factor loadings (under .40), cross-loadings, and/or low communalities (under .45) were likely to be eliminated to reduce the number of variables. Different rotating methods (e.g. orthogonal and oblique rotations) were attempted. After each component analysis, one variable was deleted, and then the component analysis was restarted with the reduced set of variables until a relatively clean set of factor loadings was achieved. The following is an example of these processes.

After the first PCA was conducted on the full set of 38 variables with orthogonal (varimax) rotation, the rotated factor matrix and communality were summarised. Visual examination identified that the highest factor loading for variable B31 was under .40, and it had cross-loadings on factor 2 (.365) and factor 4 (.387). Moreover, B31 had the smallest communality value among the variables (.420). Further analysis of the meaning of B31 ("I have had positive learning experiences") found that it was likely too general to be regarded as a reason for Chinese pre-service teachers to choose teaching as a career. For these reasons, B31 was deleted before conducting the second PCA with the reduced set of variables. The rotated factor matrix of the second component analysis showed that the total amount of variance extracted was higher than the previous time (61.5% vs. 60.8%). This verified the appropriateness of deleting B31. This process of PCA with orthogonal and oblique rotation was repeated ten times. After each of the first nine analyses, one variable was eliminated before the next analysis. The nine eliminated variables, in sequence, were B31, B20, B17, B5, B34, B8, B33, B19, and B2.

The correlation matrix and anti-image correlation pattern of the 29 revised variables, similar to those of the full set of variables, both suggested the feasibility of conducting factor analysis on the reduced set of variables. Moreover, as with the full set of variables, the reduced set of 29 variables both individually and collectively exceeded the threshold of sampling adequacy, with an overall MSA of .917. Additionally, Bartlett's test of sphericity for the reduced set of variables revealed nonzero correlations at $p = .001$. Therefore, the final principal component factor analysis with oblique rotation was conducted on the reduced 29 variables. Table 4.1 shows the explanatory power of the 29 variables expressed as eigenvalues. There were six factors with eigenvalues greater than one, the latent root criterion, which indicated that the number of factors to extract was six.

Quantitative Analysis of Chinese Pre-service Teachers' Data

Table 4.1 Extraction of Component Factors for the CCM Scale Reduced to 29 Variables

Factor	Initial Eigenvalues			Rotation Sums of Squared Loadings[a]
	Total	% of Variance	Cumulative %	Total
1	9.804	33.807	33.807	7.426
2	2.727	9.405	43.212	5.249
3	2.049	7.065	50.277	2.070
4	1.434	4.944	55.221	2.937
5	1.161	4.005	59.226	6.088
6	1.079	3.720	62.946	3.425
7	.877	3.023	65.969	
8	.856	2.951	68.920	
9	.730	2.518	71.438	
10	.700	2.413	73.851	
11	.672	2.318	76.169	
12	.627	2.161	78.330	
13	.602	2.076	80.407	
14	.560	1.932	82.339	
15	.514	1.772	84.111	
16	.483	1.666	85.777	
17	.459	1.583	87.360	
18	.420	1.447	88.807	
19	.405	1.398	90.205	
20	.374	1.288	91.493	
21	.356	1.228	92.721	
22	.337	1.161	93.882	
23	.323	1.115	94.997	
24	.303	1.046	96.043	
25	.279	.962	97.005	
26	.246	.849	97.854	
27	.235	.811	98.665	
28	.220	.759	99.424	
29	.167	.576	100.000	

Note: Extraction method is principal component analysis.
[a] When components are correlated, sums of squared loadings cannot be added to obtain a total variance.

Visual inspection of the scree plot in Figure 4.2 found that there was an "elbow" of eigenvalue between factor 6 and factor 7. Thus, both the latent root criterion (eigenvalue greater than one) and the elbow of the scree plot suggested that six factors should be retained; overall, they explained 62.9% of the variance (refer to Table 4.1).

The component factor matrix and communalities of the final principal component analysis with oblique rotation on the revised set of variables are shown in Table 4.2. As shown in the factor pattern matrix, all variables had factor loadings greater than .40, and most of them exceeded .50. This indicates that the underlying structure among the 29 variables had both statistical and practical significance of factor loadings, considering the sample size (712)

Quantitative Analysis of Chinese Pre-service Teachers' Data 55

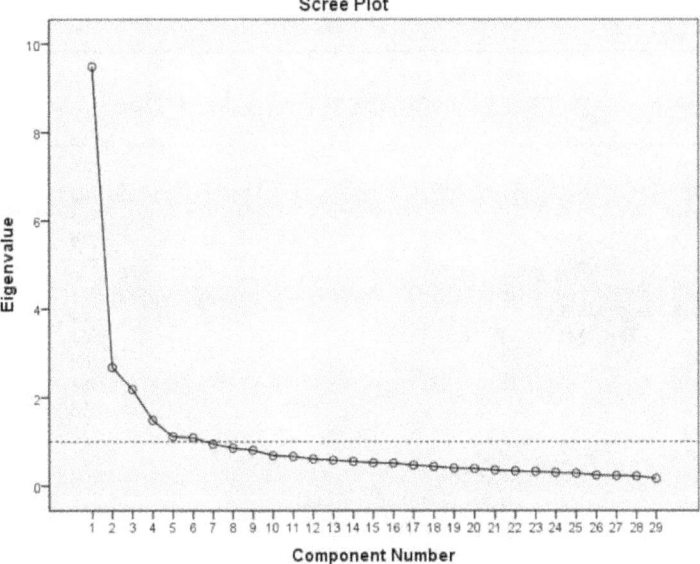

Figure 4.2 Scree Test for Component Analysis on the CCM Scale Reduced to 29 Variables

and the number of variables (Hair et al., 2010, pp. 116–118). The rightmost column shows that all variables had a communality greater than .50 except for B16, whose communality (.498) was very close to .50. This demonstrates that the variables were well accounted for by the factor solution. The factor-loading pattern had no cross-loading at the cut-off point of a factor loading greater than .40. Overall, the factor-loading matrix was clean and significant, which made the interpretation straightforward and theoretically meaningful.

The meanings of variables with significant loadings contained within each factor are demonstrated in Table 4.3. After analysing the meanings of variables in every factor, the researcher assigned a name to each factor, as shown in Table 4.3, to represent the underlying nature of the factor. Social value (altruistic motivation) refers to the social value of teaching as a career. This includes building children's characters, diminishing social disadvantages, and making contributions to social development, which stimulates pre-service teachers to choose teaching as their future career. Job advantages (extrinsic motivation) refers to the advantages of teaching as a career that are not inherent in the work itself, such as lengthy holidays, steady income, predictable working hours, job security, and a clear career path. Personal interest refers to pre-service teachers' personal interest in teaching children at school; this includes a long-lasting desire to teach and enjoyment of working with children. Teacher influence refers to positive influences from previous school

Table 4.2 Oblique-Rotated Component Analysis Pattern Matrix of the CCM Scale Reduced to 29 Variables

Variable	Factor and Factor Loading[a]						Communality
	1	2	3	4	5	6	
B38	.851						.715
B37	.807						.725
B36	.759						.665
B28	.719						.639
B9	.625						.585
B26	.620						.622
B18	.550						.573
B6	.543						.561
B23		.733					.563
B30		.705					.583
B13		.691					.616
B4		.685					.535
B24		.683					.604
B14		.648					.596
B16		.633					.498
B10			.729				.524
B27			.717				.576
B35			.625				.596
B3				.792			.672
B32				.721			.638
B21				.433			.503
B12					.744		.754
B11					.707		.756
B22					.681		.682
B29					.656		.692
B7					.639		.656
B1					.621		.686
B15						.724	.732
B25						.668	.709

Note
[a] Factor loadings below .40 have not been listed, and variables have been sorted by loadings on each factor.

teachers on pre-service teachers' choice of a teaching career. Others' suggestions refers to suggestions from important others, such as friends, classmates, and family members, and fallback career refers to teaching as a pre-service teacher's last-resort career due to limitations or difficulties in pursuing other careers. The six factors extracted from the 29 variables about teaching career choice motivation on the CCM scale, as explained before, turned out to be the six major motivations for Chinese pre-service teachers' career choices.

The reliability assessment showed that the Cronbach's alpha of the six summed scales[2] ranged from .638 to .902, and the whole summed scale had a Cronbach's alpha of .913. These measures demonstrate the acceptable internal consistency reliability of the summed scales in exploratory research (Robinson

Table 4.3 Career-Choice Motivations and Their Importance Ranking among Chinese Pre-service Teachers (N = 712)

No.	Sample Variable & Meaning	Factor Name (Types)	Summed Scale (Mean)	SD	α[a]	Rank
Factor 1	B38 Teaching will allow me to work against social disadvantage.	Social Value (Altruistic Motivation)	4.825	1.044	.902	3
	....					
Factor 2	B23 Teaching will provide a reliable income.	Job Advantages (Extrinsic Motivation)	4.907	.959	.839	2
	......					
Factor 3	B10 I was unsure of what career I wanted.	Fallback Career	3.675	1.295	.638	6
	......					
Factor 4	B3 My friends think I should become a teacher.	Others' Suggestions	4.179	1.162	.671	5
	......					
Factor 5	B12 I want a job that involves working with children/adolescents.	Personal Interest (Intrinsic Motivation)	4.655	1.223	.887	4
	......					
Factor 6	B15 I have had inspirational teachers.	Teacher Influence	5.213	1.283	.815	1
	......					

Note
[a] α stands for Cronbach's alpha, and the overall α for all 29 variables was .913. The full set of variables can be sourced from the FIT-Choice scale developed and validated by Watt and Richardson (2007).

et al., 1991). All 29 variables derived from the FIT-Choice scale were validated by the developers (Watt & Richardson, 2007) and had been reviewed and applied by many experts (Kilinc et al., 2012; Lin et al., 2012; Richardson & Watt, 2006; Watt & Richardson, 2008; Watt et al., 2012) and thus had demonstrated acceptable content validity. Moreover, as demonstrated in the factor-loading matrix (refer to Table 4.2), the clean distribution of the six significant factors suggested that the whole summed scale met the necessary level of construct validity.

Table 4.3 also shows the scores (mean values) for the summed scale for the six career-choice motivations, representing the importance that Chinese pre-service teachers placed on them. Results of paired-samples t tests showed that the summed scores for the six motivations were significantly different from each other: Teacher influence was the most important, followed by job advantages (extrinsic motivation), social value (altruistic motivation), personal interest (intrinsic motivation), others' suggestions, and fallback career.

In summary, based on the results of the quantitative data analysis, the answer to the first quantitative research question is that there are six major motivations for Chinese pre-service teachers to choose teaching as a future career, and Chinese pre-service teachers place significantly different levels of importance on each of them. The six career-choice motivations, in decreasing order of importance, are teacher influence, job advantages (extrinsic motivation), social value (altruistic motivation), personal interest (intrinsic motivation), others' suggestions, and fallback career.

4.4 Impacts of CGFTE Policy on Career-Choice Motivation of Chinese Pre-service Teachers

The second quantitative research question aimed to compare the career-choice motivations of PFPTs and SSPTs. To answer this question, the researcher used the parametric techniques of independent-samples t test and two-way between-groups ANOVA. The data analysed were collected from 712 Chinese pre-service teachers, including 309 PFPTs and 403 SSPTs, using the reduced 29-item Chinese version of the CCM scale (refer to Appendix 2). The results of these analyses shed light on the impacts of the CGFTE policy on the career-choice motivations of pre-service teachers.

4.4.1 Comparison of Career-Choice Motivation Between Policy-Funded and Self-Sponsored Pre-service Teachers

Table 4.4 shows the results of the independent-samples t-test on career-choice motivation between PFPTs and SSPTs. It shows that PFPTs placed significantly higher emphasis on personal interest as their motivation to choose the teaching profession than SSPTs (4.787 vs. 4.553, $t = 2.542$, $p < .05$). However, there were no statistical significances between the two groups for the other five career-choice motivations.

The significant difference in rankings for personal interest between PFPTs and SSPTs could be interpreted as the impact of the CGFTE policy on Chinese pre-service teachers' career-choice motivations.

4.4.2 Examining Impacts of the CGFTE Policy and Demographic Variables on Intrinsic Motivation

The existing literature indicate that demographic variables, including gender, ethnicity, home region, family income, year of study, and exam score, impact the career-choice motivations of PFPTs. Before interpreting the main effect of the CGFTE policy on career-choice motivation, it is necessary to examine the possibility of interaction effects on personal interest of the relationship between these demographic factors and the students' funding status (policy paid or self funded). To this end, the researcher conducted two-way between-groups ANOVAs on personal interest of Chinese

Table 4.4 Independent-Samples T-Test Results for the Career-Choice Motivations of PFPTs vs. SSPTs

Career-Choice Motivation	Funding Status	N	M	SD	t	df	p
Teacher Influence	PFPTs	309	5.229	1.260	.309	710	.757
	SSPTs	403	5.199	1.301			
Job Advantages (Extrinsic Motivation)	PFPTs	309	4.890	.921	−.390	710	.697
	SSPTs	403	4.919	.986			
Social Value (Altruistic Motivation)	PFPTs	309	4.829	1.067	.089	710	.929
	SSPTs	403	4.822	1.026			
Personal Interest (Intrinsic Motivation)	PFPTs	309	4.787	1.177	2.542*	710	.011
	SSPTs	403	4.553	1.248			
Others' Suggestions	PFPTs	309	4.132	1.145	−.937	710	.349
	SSPTs	403	4.215	1.174			
Fallback Career	PFPTs	309	3.601	1.316	−1.320	710	.187
	SSPTs	403	3.731	1.277			

pre-service teachers between funding status and each of the six demographic variables.

Descriptive statistics showed that the sample sizes for each demographic variable by funding status exceeded 70, except for the minority SSPTs (N = 37) and the high score group (N = 50 for PFPTs and N = 13 for SSPTs), which could provide adequate statistical power at 80% probability to identify medium or even small effects (Läuter, 1978). The univariate tests (Levene's tests) for homoscedasticity of the six designs showed that significance ranged from .238 to .648, all of which were larger than .05. Therefore, the assumption of homogeneity of variances was met (Pallant, 2013, p. 279) for the variable of personal interest in the six designs.

The results of the two-way between-groups ANOVAs showed no significant interaction effect on personal interest of the relationships between funding status and four of the six demographic variables: ethnicity, home region, family income, and exam score. Thus, it was possible to conclude that the significant main effect of funding status on personal interest was independent from the main effects of the four demographics.

4.4.2.1 Interaction Effect on Personal Interest of the Relationship Between Funding Status and Gender

The results of the between-subjects effects (refer to Table 4.5) indicate that there were statistically significant main effects on personal interest for both gender (F (1,708) = 19.876, p = .000) and funding status (F (1,708) = 5.532,

60 Quantitative Analysis of Chinese Pre-service Teachers' Data

Table 4.5 Between-Subjects Effects for Group Differences in Personal Interest Across Groups of Funding Status by Gender

Source	Type III Sum of Squares	df	Mean Square	F	Sig.	Partial $\eta 2$
Corrected Model	39.008[a]	3	13.003	8.988	.000	.037
Intercept	12834.946	1	12834.946	8871.705	0.000	.926
Gender	28.756	1	28.756	19.876	.000	.027
Funding Status	8.003	1	8.003	5.532	.019	.008
Gender × Funding Status	.002	1	.002	.001	.974	.000
Error	1024.284	708	1.447			
Total	16491.389	712				
Corrected Total	1063.291	711				

Note
[a] R Squared = .037 (Adjusted R Squared = .033)

p = .019). However, the effect sizes (partial eta squared was .027 for gender and .008 for funding status) were both small according to the guidelines suggested by Cohen (1988, p. 22) and Pallant (2013, p. 218). The results also show that there was no statistically significant interaction effect on personal interest of the relationship between gender and funding status (F (1,708) = .001, p = .974). The nonsignificant interaction effect denotes the independence of the treatments of gender and funding status; therefore, the significant main effect for each of them on personal interest can be directly interpreted.

Figure 4.3 shows the personal interest scores for male and female PFPTs and SSPTs. The almost parallel lines in the plot confirm the results of the statistical test that no interaction effects exist between gender and funding status, and the main effect of each treatment is constant at each level. Male PFPTs emphasised personal interest as their motivation to choose teaching more than male SSPTs (4.49 vs. 4.26), and female PFPTs also did so more than female SSPTs (4.92 vs. 4.70). Therefore, the impact of funding status on Chinese pre-service teachers' intrinsic career-choice motivations was independent from the influence of gender.

4.4.2.2 Interaction Effect on Personal Interest of the Relationship Between Funding Status and Year of Study

Table 4.6 displays the results indicating that there was no significant main effect for year of study on personal interest (F (1, 708) = .467, p = .494).

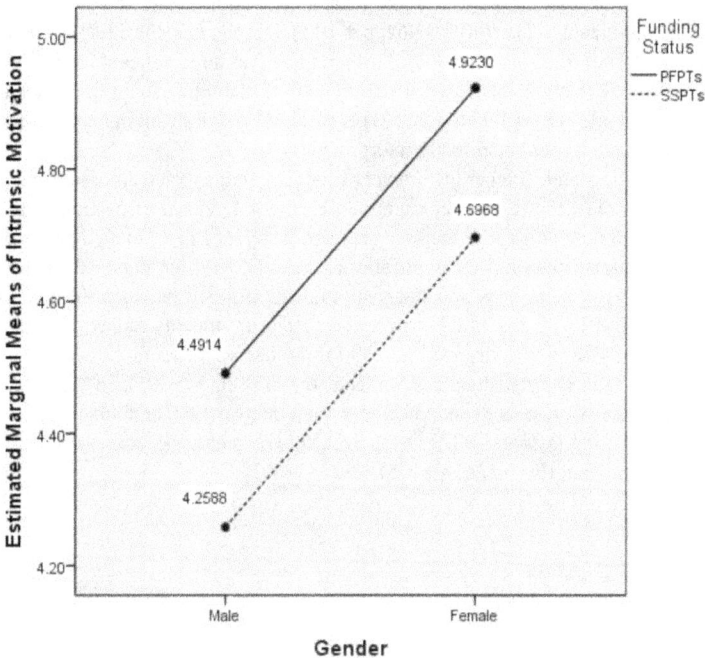

Figure 4.3 Graphical Display of Interaction Effects of Personal Interest (Intrinsic Motivation) Across Groups of Funding Status by Gender

Table 4.6 Between-Subjects Effects for Group Differences in Personal Interest Across Groups of Funding Status by Year of Study

Source	Type III Sum of Squares	df	Mean Square	F	Sig.	Partial η^2
Corrected Model	12.867[a]	3	4.289	2.891	.035	.012
Intercept	15152.460	1	15152.460	10212.959	0.000	.935
Year of Study	.693	1	.693	.467	.494	.001
Funding Status	8.821	1	8.821	5.946	.015	.008
Year of Study* Funding Status	2.894	1	2.894	1.951	.163	.003
Error	1050.424	708	1.484			
Total	16491.389	712				
Corrected Total	1063.291	711				

Note
[a] R Squared = .012 (Adjusted R Squared = .008)

However, the main effect for funding status on personal interest was statistically significant (F (1, 708) = 5.964, p = .015). Despite this, the effect size was small (partial eta squared = .008). Further, there was no significant interaction effect of the relationship between year of study and funding status on personal interest (F (1, 708) = 1.951, p = .163). Therefore, a significant main effect for funding status could be directly interpreted.

To understand whether the impact of funding status varied across different years of study, the researcher examined Figure 4.4. Visual inspection of the plot found that while both the first-year and last-year PFPTs ranked personal interest higher than did the first- and last-year SSPTs, the personal interest trends between the first- and last-year students differed between the PFPTs and the SSPTs. In the PFPT group, the first-year students ranked personal interest at 4.88, which dropped to 4.69 for the last-year PFPTs; however, this decrease was not statistically significant (t = 1.435, p > .05). In the SSPT group, the first-year students ranked personal interest 4.52, and this increased to 4.59 for the last-year SSPTs; however, this increase was also not statistically significant (t = −.526, p > .05).

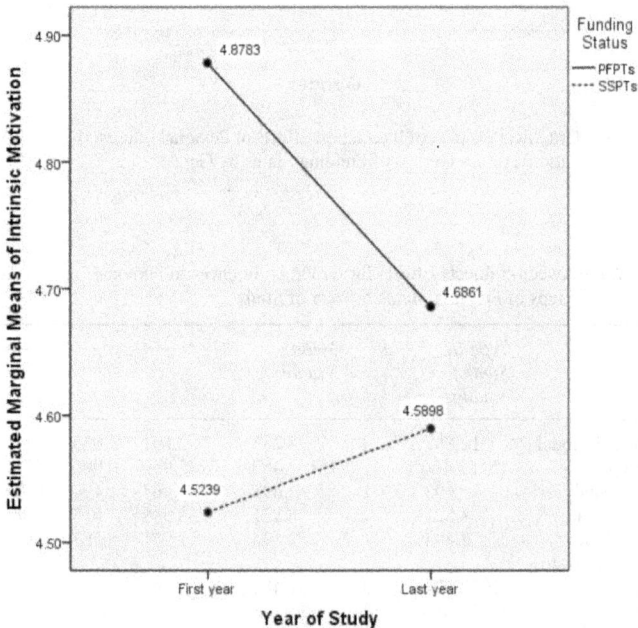

Figure 4.4 Graphical Display of Interaction Effects of Personal Interest (Intrinsic Motivation) Across Groups of Funding Status by Year of Study

Further independent-samples t tests (two-tailed) revealed that the first-year PFPTs ranked personal interest as a motivation significantly higher than did the first-year SSPTs (4.88 vs. 4.52, t = 2.784, p < .01); however, there was no significant difference in personal interest between the last-year PFPTs and SSPTs (4.69 vs. 4.59, t = .722, p > .05).

These results indicate that, compared with SSPTs, first-year PFPTs had a significantly higher intrinsic career-choice motivation. This suggests that the CGFTE policy attracted high-school graduates (the first-year PFPTs) with higher intrinsic motivation to become teachers in the form of personal interest in the career. Meanwhile, in contrast to their self-sponsored counterparts, PFPTs seem to experience a declining trend of intrinsic career-choice motivation during their four years of teacher training.

4.5 Summary of Quantitative Findings

This chapter presents a quantitative analysis of data from a questionnaire completed by policy-funded and self-sponsored pre-service teachers in China. The researcher aimed to explore the impact of the CGFTE policy on the career-choice motivations of Chinese pre-service teachers while also examining their demographic profiles. Demographic data analyses of the 712 participants from three universities in mainland China revealed that the majority of Chinese pre-service teachers are female and Han Chinese. They are typically in their early twenties and come from low-income rural families. Furthermore, comparative analyses indicate that ethnicity and socio-economic background have significant correlations with pursuing teaching at a CGFTE policy university: Specifically, a higher proportion of students with ethnic minority backgrounds were found in the policy-funded group than in the self-sponsored group. Self-funded students were more likely to come from rural and economically disadvantaged families, whereas policy-funded students had higher college entrance scores and showed greater determination to become school teachers.

The analysis of the questionnaire responses revealed six career-choice motivations, namely teacher influence, job advantages (consistent with theories of extrinsic motivation), social value (consistent with theories of altruistic motivation), personal interest (consistent with theories of intrinsic motivation), others' suggestions, and fallback career. These motivations demonstrated good psychometric qualities, and the results indicated that teacher influence was the most important career-choice factor, whereas fallback career was the least important. The students ranked job advantages, an extrinsic motivation, as second most important, and third was social value, an altruistic motivation. Personal interest, associated with intrinsic motivation, was overall rated fourth, and others' suggestions was fifth.

Among the six career-choice motivations, the PFPTs rated personal interest as significantly more important than did the SSPTs, but the two groups showed no significant differences in their rankings of the other five career-choice motivations. This result indicates that the CGFTE policy has a main effect on pre-service teachers' personal interest in teaching as an intrinsic motivation to pursue a teaching career; moreover, this main effect was significant and relatively independent of six demographic variables. However, further analyses revealed that during the four-year teacher training, those funded by the policy experienced a decline in their intrinsic career-choice motivation, while their self-sponsored counterparts experienced an increase. That is, the CGFTE policy overall appears to attract high-school graduates with higher intrinsic motivation to choose teaching as a profession, but policy-related instruction does not appear to sustain that intrinsic motivation in Chinese pre-service teachers.

Notes

1 According to an International Monetary Fund report (2013) about China's GDP, the national average monthly income in the year when the data were collected was approximately 3,000 RMB.
2 Summed scales involve combining several variables that measure the same concept into a single variable to increase the reliability of the measurement. In this study, the separate variables were combined, and their average (mean) score was used in the analysis.

References

Cohen, J. (1988). *Statistical power analysis for the behavioral sciences* (2nd ed.). Lawrence Erlbaum Associates.
Hair, J. F., Jr., Black, W. C., Babin, B. J., & Anderson, R. E. (Eds.). (2010). *Multivariate data analysis* (7th ed.). Pearson Education.
Kaiser, H. F. (1970). A second generation little jiffy. *Psychometrika, 35*(4), 401–415.
Kaiser, H. F. (1974). An index of factorial simplicity. *Psychometrika, 39*(1), 31–36.
Kaiser, H. F., & Rice, J. (1974). Little jiffy, mark IV. *Educational and Psychological Measurement, 34*(1), 111–117.
Kilinc, A., Watt, H. M. G., & Richardson, P. W. (2012). Factors influencing teaching choice in Turkey. *Asia-Pacific Journal of Teacher Education, 40*(3), 199–226.
Läuter, J. (1978). Sample size requirements for the T2 test of MANOVA (tables for one-way classifications). *Biometrical Journal, 20*, 389–406.
Lin, E., Shi, Q.-M., Wang, J., Zhang, S.-A., & Liu, H. (2012). Initial motivations for teaching: Comparison between preservice teachers in the United States and China. *Asia-Pacific Journal of Teacher Education, 40*(3), 227–248.
Pallant, J. (2013). *SPSS survival manual: A step by step guide to data analysis using IBM SPSS* (5th ed.). Allen & Unwin.
Richardson, P. W., & Watt, H. M. G. (2006). Who chooses teaching and why? Profiling characteristics and motivations across three Australian universities. *Asia-Pacific Journal of Teacher Education, 34*(1), 27–56.
Robinson, J. P., Shaver, P. R., & Wrightsman, L. S. (1991). Criteria for scale selection and evaluation. In J. P. Robinson, P. R. Shaver, & L. S. Wrightsman (Eds.), *Measures of personality and social psychological attitudes*. Academic Press.

Watt, H. M. G., & Richardson, P. W. (2007). Motivational factors influencing teaching as a career choice: Development and validation of the FIT-choice scale. *The Journal of Experimental Education, 75*(3), 167–202.

Watt, H. M. G., & Richardson, P. W. (2008). Motivations, perceptions, and aspirations concerning teaching as a career for different types of beginning teachers. *Learning and Instruction, 18*(5), 408–428.

Watt, H. M. G., Richardson, P. W., Klusmann, U., Kunter, M., Beyer, B., Trautwein, U., & Baumert, J. (2012). Motivations for choosing teaching as a career: An international comparison using the FIT-Choice scale. *Teaching and Teacher Education, 28*(6), 791–805.

5 Narrative Stories of Ten Policy-Funded Pre-Service Teachers and Reflections

Introduction

This chapter presents the reflective thoughts and perspectives of ten PFPTs in narrative form to explore answers to the qualitative research question posed in the present study: "How do PFPTs with different attitudes towards the CGFTE policy explain their motivations for choosing teaching as their future career?" It begins with a brief introduction of the ten interviewees who participated in this qualitative study through online audio interviews. The narrative stories of the ten PFPTs were compiled, and each story comprises the complex and often challenging process of deciding to apply for teacher-education majors before attending university, influenced by various factors. The stories are classified into three groups according to the students' satisfaction with the CGFTE policy, representing the voices of different PFPTs. Analyses of these stories of the PFPTs demonstrate the complexity of their career-choice motivations and provide an illustrative complement to the quantitative findings in this study.

5.1 Demographic Information of Participants

The ten interviewees (refer to Table 5.1) were PFPTs enrolled at University A who had previously participated in questionnaire surveys. Three of them (Rui Hao, Meng Meng, and Ming Mei) were interviewed online in 2022, while the other seven interviewees participated in online interviews in 2013. All but one (Zhen Zhen) identified themselves as part of the Han majority. Based on their satisfaction with different terms of the CGFTE policy, as rated on a seven-point Likert scale, the ten PFPTs were classified into high, medium, and low satisfaction groups.

5.2 Voices From the High-Satisfaction Group

5.2.1 Becoming a Kindergarten Teacher Out of Personal Interest: The Story of Li Wen

Li Wen, 20 years old at the time of the 2013 interview, hailed from a rural area in Sichuan Province, China, with a family income of approximately 4,000 RMB

Table 5.1 Demographic Information of the Ten Interviewees

Pseud.	Age	Gen.	Hom.	Mon. Fam. Inc. (RMB)	Uni. Maj.	Year of Stu.	Pol.-Sat. Lev. (M) Enc. Terms	Pol.-Sat. Lev. (M) Rest. Terms
Li Wen	20	F	Rur.	4,000	Pre-sch. Edu.	2nd	7.00	6.40
Da Wu	21	M	Rur.	2,000	Math Edu.	2nd	7.00	5.80
Xiao Fang	19	F	Urb.	4,000	Che. Edu.	2nd	6.00	5.40
Ming Mei	18	F	Rur.	4,000	Eng. Edu.	2nd	5.71	5.71
Zhen Zhen	22	F	Rur.	2,500	Eng. Edu.	2nd	6.14	3.80
Wen Jing	19	F	Urb.	/	Che. Edu.	2nd	6.00	3.60
Rui Hao	17	M	Urb.	10,000	Edu. Tech.	1st	5.71	4.71
Bin Bin	20	M	Rur.	3,000	Pre-sch. Edu.	2nd	5.43	1.60
Zhu Min	20	F	Rur.	5,000	Che. Edu.	2nd	2.57	2.20
Meng Meng	18	F	Urb.	6,000	Edu. Tech.	1st	5.71	3.14

per month. Her score on the NCEE was 26 points higher than the admission score for first-class universities set by Sichuan Province. As such, she was admitted as a PFPT majoring in pre-school education at University A. Li Wen stated that she planned to teach children in a kindergarten after graduation. Li Wen completed the whole process of choosing her major and university herself. She researched information and selected the major of pre-school education based on her own interests:

> I still remember when we were filling out university application forms soon after graduating from high school. Our school sent us many brochures introducing universities and majors. Some of my school teachers told me that my score on the NCEE seemed to meet the requirements of University A. At that time, I wasn't familiar with how to fill out the form, so I took all the brochures back home. I read the brochures repeatedly to see which universities and majors I could apply for. When I opened a brochure and turned to the page introducing University A, I paid close attention to the majors. There were majors like English, pre-school education, etc. I was very interested in teaching in kindergarten, and I knew that graduates in the major of pre-school education would become kindergarten teachers. Without any hesitation, I put the major of pre-school education as my first choice on the application form to University A. My parents didn't object to my decision, and luckily, I was admitted to the university.

Li Wen was interested in kindergarten teaching for several reasons. She was familiar with the profession, enjoyed the working environment at kindergarten, and, most importantly, liked children:

> I think my interest in teaching at a kindergarten was aroused by three factors. Firstly, I have a cousin who is a kindergarten teacher in Chengdu. She

told me many stories about what happened in that kindergarten. Sometimes I went to that kindergarten and played games with children there. Through these experiences, I accumulated knowledge about the profession. . . . Secondly, I like the working environment of kindergarten. It is simple and pure, which is quite different from many other professions. Nowadays, it is well-known that the working environment of many professions in China is very "complicated" due to the emphasis on interpersonal relationships in Chinese culture. Personally, I don't like that working condition because it is very easy to get into trouble. However, the working environment of kindergarten is relatively simple, and there is no "battle of wits and courage" or "intrigue against each other" in kindergarten. The annoyance of kindergarten teachers, if they have any, is usually caused by the naughtiness of kids and often disappears quickly. I think that kind of simplicity in kindergarten is good.

Last but not least, I like children very much. I still remember what happened several years ago when I met a group of kindergarten kids for the first time. That day, my cousin invited me to meet her at the kindergarten where she was teaching. When I arrived, the class had just ended. Many children were waiting in the classroom for their parents to take them home, and my cousin was standing in front of them. As soon as I entered the classroom, some kids asked my cousin simultaneously, "Miss Zhang, who's she?" One child put up his small right hand to get my attention and asked me, "Teacher, what's your name please?" After I answered their questions, many kids raised their hands and told me, "Miss Li, I want to sing a song to you". I said to them, "That will be great! Can you please sit down? You can sing songs one after another, okay?" Although it was our first meeting, they listened to me carefully and followed my instructions to sit down quietly before starting to sing a song one after another. Their voices were very loud, and I felt so happy. . . . I often went to that kindergarten afterwards, and they never regarded me as a stranger or intruder. When I played games with them on the playground, they treated me as one of their teachers. When I guided them outside of the kindergarten to eat ice cream, they treated me as their good friend. On weekends, if they met me at the park, they would not call me teacher, but "Mommy". Sometimes they may become naughty and noisy, but they were always attached to me, and we gradually became good friends.

Li Wen's personality was also suited towards being a kindergarten teacher:

> I think if I become a kindergarten teacher, children will like my personality. I am vivacious, cheerful, and funny. I have a happy smile and a sweet voice. Although I am 20 years old, I act like a child when doing things. All the kids living around my house like me very much. Once I come back home, they will come and ask me to play games with them. When I talk

with them, I make them laugh. I join in all their activities and enjoy them: I watch the cartoons they watch; I can sing almost all the songs they sing; I tutor them when they are doing their homework. I never refuse their invitations to play games with them. For example, if they ask me to do rope skipping, I will do it with them, and I never say, "Oh no, that's childish". Therefore, it is impossible for children to exclude me from their activities.

The CGFTE policy seemed to have no decisive influence on Li Wen's choice of becoming a kindergarten teacher. However, the consistency between the restrictive policy terms and Li Wen's expectations on professional development reinforced her determination to choose teaching:

> I knew about the CGFTE policy when I selected my major and university. I think the policy had only a slight influence on my choice of teaching in kindergarten as a career, but I don't think it had a final say on my decision. My ideas were very simple: if you want to become a teacher, it goes without doubt that the policy will help you a lot. The policy terms say that graduates must teach for a minimum of six years, but for a person like me who wants to teach for twenty years or even for their whole life, that is not a problem at all. One difference between the SSPTs and the PFPTs may be that the former can teach in other provinces, but the latter cannot. However, for me, that is not a problem. I think there is no big difference between my home province of Sichuan and other provinces. And I like to teach in Sichuan, even though it is in the southwest part of China. Many people think that big cities in coastal provinces provide them with a better developmental platform. Even if they are right, I think that if too many people flock into coastal provinces, the fierce competition there will make even talented people feel great pressure. This is just like what usually happens at schools. A student with high exam scores in an ordinary class is transferred to a top class in the hope that they will receive better education and hence achieve higher scores. However, it often turns out that their scores become lower and lower because they feel too much pressure from other students in the top class.

5.2.2 Job Advantages, Social Value, and Others' Suggestions as Career-Choice Motivations: The Story of Da Wu

Da Wu was a second-year male undergraduate majoring in mathematics education at University A. Born and raised in a rural area in Jiangxi Province of China, he came from a relatively poor family with a monthly income of about 2,000 RMB. As a PFPT majoring in mathematics education, he would become a math teacher in a senior high school after graduation. Da Wu had low self-efficacy for pursuing many jobs except for teaching. Teaching as a profession, according to his understanding, had many advantages over other jobs: easy to get started, free of pressure, and full of free time. These advantages increased his sense of competence in taking up the profession:

> I am afraid I don't have enough capacity to work in many jobs. Working as a bank clerk or a doctor, for example, would make me feel stressed. When I stay with adults, I'm used to thinking about what they really want to do and what their purposes are for approaching me. However, I think teaching as a profession is quite different. I was once a school student before attending university, and I know students are pure in thought. So, I will feel relaxed if the people I work for in my future career are students. Although teaching as a career for a man is not as profitable as other professions, I think teaching is comparatively easy, and it is well-known that teachers have a lot of free time, including two long holidays every year.

The social value of teaching was another motivational factor for Da Wu to choose teaching as a career. He had a strong desire to help children succeed, and gaining respect from both students and parents for his teaching was something he valued:

> I like the feeling of teaching children what I have learned, and I cherish the experience of teaching others. As a PFPT, I must teach for six years. I hope all my students during that period will graduate and be equipped with useful knowledge and skills for society. I am looking forward to that enjoyable and rewarding experience. When I was a student, I admired those teachers who had personal charm. If I become a teacher, I will try my best to become a good teacher with personal charm and help my students improve their academic achievements. Then, I will be respected and admired by my students, and their parents will give me good reviews as well. Just imagining that makes me feel so good.

In Da Wu's final stage of choosing a major and university, his uncle analysed the benefits of choosing a teacher-training program at University A. The suggestion from his uncle coincided with Da Wu's own view and reinforced his decision to become a teacher:

> I have an uncle who is a school teacher. He is a knowledgeable and considerate person who knows the teaching profession very well. When it came to choosing a major and university on the application form, he recommended the mathematics education major at University A. He said that University A was a national key university with moderate requirements for NCEE scores. My score was not high enough to go to some of the top national universities, but it should meet the requirements of University A. He further analysed that the university was very strong in the mathematics education major; therefore, graduates in that major could easily find a

good teaching job in a decent school. I fully agreed with my uncle, and I thought what he said was very reasonable. If I chose that major, I would become a math teacher, and that was what I wanted to be. So, I made up my mind and put mathematics education as the major on the application form submitted to University A. Finally, I was accepted as a PFPT here at University A.

When Da Wu chose his major and university, the CGFTE policy met his needs and fuelled his inclination to choose teaching as a career:

> I didn't know about the CGFTE policy until my uncle introduced it to me when I was filling out the university application form. After reading it, I realized it was implemented by six universities, including University A. I think the stipulations of the policy are really good and appropriate for me. I don't think I can do other jobs well, but I am sure that I can teach well. The policy just assures that I will be a teacher anyway.

5.2.3 Others' Suggestions, Personal Interest, and Job Advantages as Career-Choice Motivations: The Story of Xiao Fang

Xiao Fang was a second-year PFPT majoring in chemistry education at University A. She came from an urban area in Guangdong Province of China, and her family's monthly income was about 4,000 RMB. After graduation from university, she would become a chemistry teacher at a senior high school. However, she had not decided to become a school teacher until it came to choosing a major at university.

Xiao Fang had many different ideas about what to do when she was a little girl, but she did not make up her mind to teach until she graduated from high school. Her choice of becoming a school teacher was mainly influenced by suggestions from her parents, relatives, and teachers:

> Most of my classmates do not think carefully about what careers they will pursue in the future. Slightly different from them, when I was a child, I had imagined what to do after I grew up, for example, to be a lawyer, a doctor, etc. However, those ideas were all "day-dreams". I didn't have a definite answer to the question of what to do in the future until it came to filling out the college entrance application form. . . . At that critical moment, I talked with my parents about which university and major to choose. My father suggested that I apply for a teacher-training university because he thought there were many benefits for a female to become a teacher. My mother held the same opinion and cited the good living conditions of my aunt, who was a school teacher, as an example to support my father's idea.

I was also told by one of my head-teachers at the senior high school that her daughter enrolled in a teacher-training program at University A.

Xiao Fang ultimately embraced the suggestion to become a teacher because she had a personal interest in teaching and believed in the advantages of teaching as a career, as well as the benefits of the CGFTE policy:

> Many of my relatives were teachers. Based on their experiences and living conditions, I agreed that teaching as a profession had many advantages. The profession was stable and had fixed long holidays. Compared with workers at companies, teachers at school were able to enjoy more free time in life. I did not hate teaching actually; instead, I had a positive attitude towards it and felt interested in school teaching. Last and most importantly, under the current situation of difficulty in job hunting, the policy term that guaranteed a teaching job for graduates of PFPTs was very attractive. So, I finally took their suggestion and put chemistry education as the major at University A on the application form. Luckily, I was accepted.

5.2.4 Mixed Motivations to Choose Teaching: The Story of Ming Mei

Ming Mei was an 18-year-old second-year PFPT when the online interview was conducted in 2022. She came from a rural area of Chongqing with a relatively poor family background. As her university major was English education, she planned to become an English teacher at a junior or senior high school after graduation. The factors that influenced Ming Mei's choice of teaching were various. Among them, the motivations that she emphasised most were the social value of teaching and her personal interest:

> I had many dreams when I was a child, and the one that I want to realise the most is to become a teacher. I think teaching as a profession is really important, and its value is immeasurable. Through words and deeds, teachers can pass on their knowledge and life experience to students. To realise the value of my life, I hope in the future I can guide students to learn knowledge and to change for the better. . . . My teachers had very positive influences on me. I love the profession of teaching, and becoming a teacher does not hinder me from developing other interests or hobbies.

Additionally, suggestions from a teacher, the CGFTE policy itself, and teaching as a fallback career also played vital roles in her decision to pursue teaching:

> When it came time to choose my university major, I was considering teacher education and mass media, and I had to select one of them.

Considering the heavy pressure on media workers, I decided to choose the major of teacher education. But which university should I choose? When I was hesitating between University W and University A, one of my senior high school teachers influenced my decision. She asked me to think about what I would like to do after graduation from university. "If you want to become a teacher", she suggested, "then it's better to study at University A because it is a top-ranking teacher-training university where you can acquire professional skills to enhance the possibility of success in your future teaching career". I wish for my parents to lead a relaxed life, and I don't want to add to their financial burden by paying for my tuition fees. The CGFTE policy just meets my needs. . . . What's more, my scores on the NCEE were not as high as I expected, which may not meet the requirements of my ideal university. To avoid the risk of being rejected, I decided to select a teacher-education program at University A, whose enrolment mark was not too high. As a result, I put University A on my university application form and selected English education, one of the teacher-education programs supported by the CGFTE policy, as my university major. . . . Now, I am studying at University A, and I think it is not a bad result because University A is an excellent university.

5.3 Voices From the Medium-Satisfaction Group

5.3.1 Policy Attraction and Teacher Influence as Decisive Career-Choice Motivations: The Story of Zhen Zhen

Zhen Zhen was a second-year PFPT majoring in English education at University A. After graduation, she planned to become an English teacher at a high school, but she had not expected to become a teacher when she was a high school student. Several reasons led her to choose teaching as her future career. Among these reasons, the attraction of the CGFTE policy and the examples of previous role model teachers were the decisive factors. Initially, Zhen Zhen wanted to work in a high-paying job, and she had no interest in teaching for a long time:

When I was a child, I didn't want to become a teacher. Even when I was in high school or just graduated from high school, I didn't expect to become a teacher. One reason was that as a student from a poor rural area, I hoped to become rich. So, I wanted to choose a major that could help me work in a big company with a high salary. The other reason was that I didn't like jobs such as teaching that had no variety or changes. If I became a teacher after graduation, I would have to teach and stay in a school and probably could not change workplaces, and I could predict what would happen in the next decades. I just didn't like such a stereotyped working mode.

Zhen Zhen's friends suggested teaching as a career when it came time to choose a major at university. She valued the advantages of teaching as a career recommended by her friends, and by this time, she had developed some interest in teaching, which also played a role:

> As an ethnic minority student, I had the opportunity to study at University A for one year of foundation courses before applying to become an undergraduate at the same university. After completing the foundation courses, I had to apply for a major at the university like everyone else. At that time, I discovered there were many teacher-preparation programs which I was not aware of before. So, I asked for suggestions from my friends who were pre-service teachers at the university. They told me about the various advantages of teaching as a career. I knew their advice was just advice, and I had to make the final decision. I considered their suggestions and realised that becoming a teacher actually had some advantages that catered to my needs. Firstly, it was comparatively easy to find a teaching job currently. Secondly, teaching as a stable job suited female graduates well. Thirdly, teachers had such long holidays. Moreover, although I still didn't particularly like it, I had a little interest in the profession of teaching at that time.

Ultimately, Zhen Zhen's decision to become a teacher was driven by financial pressures. Living in a poor family in a rural area of China, Zhen Zhen was greatly influenced by Chinese traditional culture. She did not want her education to cost her parents too much money. An unexpected car accident that occurred in her poor family made their financial situation even worse. At that critical moment, the CGFTE policy gave her a ray of hope, and she finally decided to become a PFPT:

> I am the daughter of a poor family in an ethnic minority community. As a female, I prefer not to be too involved in society and would rather stay at home to take care of my family. Additionally, I want to relieve my parents' financial burden by minimizing their tuition fees. Although the government and society openly oppose sex discrimination, families usually tend to invest more in their sons than daughters. The main reason is that when a daughter gets married, she will move out to join her husband's family and live there. Therefore, I personally do not want my parents to spend too much money on my education. . . . Just a few months before I graduated from high school, a terrible car accident happened to my father. The expensive medical expenses put my poor family under a mountain of debt. I did not want to add any more pressure on them by asking for tuition fees. Fortunately, I learned about the CGFTE policy, and I knew that undergraduates in this program would be free of all fees at the university. That was great news for me, as I can save my parents money if I enrol in it. Therefore, I made up my mind and chose English education as my major on the application form for University A.

Narrative Stories of Ten Policy-Funded Pre-Service Teachers 75

Zhen Zhen's choice of teaching was also influenced by her previous school teachers. She had many positive experiences with teachers when she was in junior high school. Her teachers acted as role models, encouraging her to become a good student:

> When I was a junior high school student, many teachers liked me very much. They said I was a smart, honest, hardworking, and lovely young lady who always scored high on exams. After being elected as the class monitor, I had more opportunities to talk with teachers. All those positive experiences with teachers increased my interest in studying during junior high school education. I still remember how hard I studied when the senior high school entrance examination was around the corner. I attended every evening class during that period and came back home very late. Usually, my family was watching TV when I arrived home, but instead of joining them for entertainment, I went directly to my study room and continued studying until midnight. Therefore, I have had strong self-study abilities ever since. Moreover, I was able to concentrate so well in class that I could write down over 90% of what the teacher had taught. Our physics teacher once tested our concentration in class by conducting an exam among students immediately after finishing the class. I got a full mark on that test.

Zhen Zhen mentioned two school teachers in particular who left a deep impression on her. What they had done greatly influenced her career-choice motivation:

> There were two teachers in my junior high school who left me with lasting impressions. They both had a strong sense of responsibility and cared for students deeply. I was moved by what they had done, and I hoped to become a good teacher like them. One was my English teacher. He would often raise questions in class, and the teaching and learning atmosphere in his classroom was relaxed. All my classmates developed an interest in studying English; nobody was forced to learn it. I was extremely active in his class and often volunteered to answer his questions. Every afternoon after the radio exercises, he used his spare time to give me and another student free tutoring, such as correcting errors in our exams. He invested a lot in our education, and we respected him very much. The other was my physics teacher. She was one of the few female physics teachers in our school. Teachers who taught physics were usually regarded as talented people with high IQs. Therefore, we all admired her. As a teacher of a class preparing to take the entrance examination for senior high schools, she was very strict and responsible. During that critical period, many wealthy parents paid a lot of money to send their children to good private cram schools in the hope that their children would receive extra tutoring and hence score high on the entrance exam. Our physics teacher bought many teaching materials, including entrance examination papers from previous

years, and she gave the entire class free tutoring. Sometimes, she even initiated extra free tutoring for some excellent students. We knew she had very high expectations for us. She hoped that we would all be able to score high and be accepted into key senior high schools. The longer she was our teacher, the more we respected and liked her.

However, after becoming a pre-service teacher at university, Zhen Zhen realised that her school teachers personally did not want her to become a teacher because they had "very high expectations" for their excellent students' future career development:

> My school teachers didn't know that I had chosen to become a school teacher in the first place. After I attended University A, I contacted my school teachers, including the two I mentioned above, and told them that I was a PFPT. They were all somewhat surprised. They didn't expect me to become a teacher. I felt upset when I heard their responses, but I quickly calmed down because I knew the reasons for their reactions. In their view, it was very difficult for students in rural area schools to get high scores on the NCEE. The students who were able to pass the exam and be accepted by national key universities were excellent students in their eyes, and they had very high expectations for those students' future development. Moreover, most people in society, including my teachers, believed that working in a large enterprise paved the way for employees' promotion and career development. Teaching in a school, however, was deemed by them as a profession that lacked potential prospects. They thought that for the self-sponsored pre-service teachers, they still had the chance to become an academic postgraduate and change their direction of development, but for the PFPTs, they had no choice but to become a school teacher.

Fortunately, as a PFPT, Zhen Zhen's determination to become a school teacher did not seem to be shaken by her previous teachers' views. The social value of teaching held great importance to her, as she stated:

> I personally do not agree with my school teachers' ideas. I believe that the rewards of teaching are more than just financial compensation. As the old Chinese saying goes, being a teacher can "impart knowledge, cultivate people, and have students everywhere". The respect and gratitude from students are what I look forward to the most. I believe that I can achieve self-fulfilment and self-affirmation by teaching students in a school. Despite the various problems in education that are complained about by many people in China, I want to become a good teacher who can educate children and contribute to improving the current education situation.

5.3.2 Others' Suggestions and Job Advantages as Career-Choice Motivations: The Story of Wen Jing

Wen Jing was a second-year PFPT at University A, majoring in chemistry education. After graduating from university, she was going to become a chemistry teacher at a high school. However, she chose to become a teacher by chance.

Wen Jing had not decided on her future career when she was at school. When it came to choosing a university major, she rashly made the decision to become a school chemistry teacher. Her career-choice motivation was influenced by suggestions from others and the advantages of teaching as a career for females:

> When I was studying at school, I had different dreams for my future career, such as becoming a doctor, a nurse, a scientist, etc. However, I was not against becoming a teacher. After graduated from high school, we had to choose a major at university on the university application form. One day I was invited by my best friend to go to her home for dinner. I accepted her invitation and arrived at her place a little early. When I entered her house, I saw that she was filling out the application form. Her father was standing beside her and giving suggestions. We chatted for a while about which major and university we should choose. Her father introduced University A to us and then required us to carefully read about the CGFTE policy. Finally, her father asked if we would like to become teachers. My friend said that if I chose a teacher-training program, she would choose the same program too. . . . We were very good friends and cherished our friendship very much. If we studied at the same university, we were able to help each other and maintain our friendship. Additionally, I thought teaching was a suitable career for females. It was a comparatively easy job with long vacations. Teachers were able to take care of their families because they could come back home after completing several classes at school. So, both of us chose the major of chemistry education at University A on the application form. Luckily, we were both accepted by the university and became PFPTs.

5.3.3 Personal Interest, Other's Suggestions, and Fallback Career as Career-Choice Motivations: The Story of Rui Hao

Born into a relatively affluent family, 17-year-old Rui Hao was a freshman at University A. He was studying educational technology in a teacher-training program funded by the CGFTE policy and knew he would become an ICT teacher at a senior high school. Rui Hao's experience indicated that he was motivated by various factors to choose teaching as a career, including his personal interest in teaching, suggestions from his father and school teachers, and teaching as a fallback career:

> I have had the dream of becoming a teacher since I was a junior high school student. I used to teach my classmates how to solve complex math problems if I understood them well. So, I think I am suitable for the teaching profession. . . . The process of filling out my university application was quite complicated. When I was a high school student, I got good grades and always wanted to apply for the national top-ranking normal universities, such as BNU or ECNU. Unfortunately, I didn't perform well on the NCEE, and the scores I received were not high enough for me to be accepted into the universities I hoped for. I was disappointed and was thinking of taking the exams again the next year. However, it was time-consuming and tiring, and all my friends, relatives, and teachers suggested that I not attend the exams again the following year because there would be more high school graduates and the university application competition would be fiercer. My father, who is a teacher, also told me that the government attached great importance to teachers, and nowadays teachers were well-paid and respected by society. After careful consideration, I decided to directly apply to some teacher-training universities whose requirements were not very high. Among them, University A was my first choice due to its location and reputation. So, I filled out the University A application form and selected majors such as math education, physics education, and others. Finally, as a result of competition, I was accepted into the major of educational technology – a teacher-training program at University A funded by the CGFTE policy.

5.4 Voices From the Low-Satisfaction Group

5.4.1 Teaching as a Fallback Career Choice: The Story of Bin Bin

Bin Bin was one of the few male pre-service teachers who majored in pre-school education at University A. However, becoming a kindergarten teacher was not his first choice. Bin Bin seemed to know little about pre-school education before attending university. His original intention was to study civil engineering at university, so he made a lot of preparations in that area while in high school. When it came to applying to universities and choosing majors after graduating from high school, Bin Bin originally put two non-teacher-training universities on his application form:

> My score on the NCEE was around 20 points higher than the basic score required by my home province for national key universities. I thought my

score might not be high enough for some national top universities. But at the very beginning, I still insisted on choosing SCU and UEST in my application form because they were the top universities I had always dreamed of.

However, just a few days before officially submitting his application form, he changed his mind after learning about an additional choice. As the son of a relatively poor family in a rural area of Sichuan Province, Bin Bin wanted to release his family's financial burden of covering his university tuition fees by becoming a PFPT. The CGFTE policy at University A catered to his needs and played an important role in his decision to attend the teacher-training program:

> I received a notice to go back to our high school just five days before submitting the university application form. When we gathered at the school, our teachers told us about a preferential admission scheme for those who wanted to become a PFPT in one of the six teacher training universities that were implementing the CGFTE policy. I learned that if candidates' scores on the NCEE reached the requirement set by the policy university, they would be recruited as a pre-service teacher with full government funding for four-year undergraduate studies. That was exactly what I needed. My parents do not earn much, even though they work hard. I always want to share the financial burden with them. By joining the scheme, I am able to save a large sum of money for my family. I also learned that University A was one of the six policy universities carrying out the scheme and had a relatively lower entrance score requirement. So, finally, I selected University A and prioritized it by putting it ahead of my previous two universities on my application form.

In September 2012, Bin Bin was admitted to University A. He was "surprised" when he learned that pre-school education was the major he was going to study at University A:

> I think my study of pre-school education was a pure "accident", and I was surprised when I first learned it was my major at university. I was a science student in high school, and my original goal was to become an engineer. So, the majors I chose on my application form to University A were primarily related to science and technology. Pre-school education was actually the last major I listed on the form. Unfortunately, because my college entrance exam score failed to meet the requirement of science or technology teacher preparation programs in University A, I was registered in the pre-school teacher education program, which had a relatively low requirement for the score due to its difficulty in recruiting students.

Facing social dissuasion and considering the difficulties of being a male kindergarten teacher, Bin Bin had a plan for his professional development: to become a kindergarten teacher soon after graduation and ultimately to establish a kindergarten under his own management:

> My parents were disappointed when they learned I was majoring in preschool education and would become a kindergarten teacher after graduation. Many of my relatives, friends, and neighbours simply cannot understand my choice because they think it is a waste of talent for a male to become a kindergarten teacher. They think I should become an engineer or a doctor since I was a science student in high school. . . . I personally do not agree with them. I think pre-school education as a major is essential for the nation's development. At the same time, I also understand how difficult it is for a man to become a kindergarten teacher. For example, it is inconvenient and even embarrassing for a male kindergarten teacher to handle certain tasks that a female teacher may find easy. Living and teaching in a kindergarten dominated by female teachers could make male teachers feel isolated or even lonely. The possible psychological problems for male kindergarten teachers are what I deeply concern. Therefore, I plan to do something related to education after graduation, but I will not necessarily become a kindergarten teacher. My plan is to first study hard on the major at the university, then teach at a kindergarten after graduation to learn more practical skills, and finally realize my goal of establishing my own kindergarten.

5.4.2 Fallback Career, Others' Suggestions, and Job Advantages as Career-Choice Motivations: The Story of Zhu Min

Zhu Min was a second-year PFPT studying chemistry education at University A, which meant she was going to become a school chemistry teacher after graduation. However, teaching chemistry at school was not her original plan. When it came time to decide what to study at the university, Zhu Min initially wanted to choose the major she was most interested in. But after learning about the employment situation, she became indecisive about her original plan:

> I was interested in architecture design when I was in high school. My original plan was to study civil engineering at the university. As soon as I learned that I had an excellent score on the NCEE, I started to gather information about the civil engineering major, especially about the employment situation for graduates in the field. My parents and aunts also helped me to learn more about it. One day, while searching online, I repeatedly found astonishing information: After a job interview with a group of graduates majoring in civil engineering, employers would rather give an offer to a

male graduate who failed several courses at the university than employ an excellent female graduate. It saddened me so much that I felt like being punched in the head. I asked myself, "Should I give it up?"

At the same time, Zhu Min's plan to become a female civil engineer was disapproved of by her parents and other relatives. They suggested that she consider other majors:

> Almost all my family members told me that studying civil engineering was not a good idea. My parents said that civil engineers had to work at construction sites, and after completing work at one site, they had to move along with the construction team to work at another new site. My aunt cited some examples of her friends who were civil engineers to support my parents' idea. They concluded that the work without a stable living place was not suitable for a female and advised me to become a doctor or a teacher.

In Zhu Min's opinion, teaching as a career had many advantages over being a doctor, such as an "easy and interesting job", "long holidays", and "respect from students and parents":

> Compared to being a doctor, I think teaching is a better career choice because being a teacher has many unique advantages. I think teaching is a relatively easy job. My aunt is a school teacher, and every time I visited her, she seemed to be sitting in her office at ease, looking very free. Additionally, teachers enjoy long summer and winter holidays every year and are still paid during these holidays. Even during the school year, teaching different children can enrich a teacher's life. No two students are the same, and they have different ideas every day. Teaching them can make life full of fun. If teachers teach their students well, they will be respected by both their students and their parents. Just imagine the scenario of students visiting their teachers during these holidays! The teachers must enjoy it very much.

Influenced by her family members' advice and attracted by the advantages of teaching, Zhu Min finally decided to change her mind and take her family members' suggestions. She selected chemistry education as her first choice on the university application form.

> At last, I decided to take my parents' suggestion and become a teacher. After all, parents would never harm their own children, right? There was a column at the top of the university application form for selecting national key teacher-training universities. It was an additional chance for choosing national key universities, but if it was filled out, candidates may lose the

chance to go to other comprehensive universities. I didn't want to waste it. So, I filled out that column with the major of chemistry education at University A. Luckily, my application was approved, and I was admitted as a PFPT.

Zhu Min added that the CGFTE policy had slightly influenced her choice of major:

> I knew all the CGFTE policy terms before filling out my university application form. I think the policy, to say the least, had a little influence on my choice of major. I thought it restricted candidates too much. But the term stipulating that we have to come back to our home province to teach was consistent with my plan. If I teach in other provinces, I can only visit my parents on long holidays. Teaching at a school close to my family, however, will make visiting my parents much easier and more convenient.

5.4.3 Mixed Motivations to Choose Teaching: The Story of Meng Meng

As a new university student majoring in educational technology and funded by the policy, Meng Meng believed that she would become a school teacher teaching ICT or chemistry after graduation. In fact, many factors attracted her to choose the teaching profession:

> I had a dream of becoming a teacher when I was a junior high school student. I got along well with my classmates and teachers at school, and they treated me very well too. In my daily life, I prefer crowded and noisy environments filled with people, and I enjoy working with students. My parents and relatives all think that teaching is a suitable profession for me. . . . Comparatively speaking, schools are a pure place where meeting with teachers and classmates is easy and relaxing. I think this is an advantage of teaching and a reason for me to choose teaching. Teachers are models for students, and they can truly influence a student or even a whole class of students. The words and deeds of a teacher can bring students something powerful. I think I can also pass something valuable on to students if I become a teacher. . . . Surely, teachers nowadays usually bear heavy pressure. This is especially true for head teachers at high schools when their students suffer from study burden and need guidance. But I think people should treat it dialectically as all professions have two sides. . . . When I was in my second year of high school, I told my parents that I would apply for a teacher-training university. However, University A was not my goal at that time because I was afraid that my score was not high enough to apply for it. Luckily, I did exceptionally well and received a very high score on the NCEE, which was beyond my wildest dream. So, I

was certain to apply for a policy-funded teacher-training program at University A. My parents supported my new plan, and we then began to search for more information about the CGFTE policy. Finally, I was successfully accepted into University A but, as my score was just above the bar of the university, I was adjusted to the major of educational technology that few students applied for.

5.5 Reflections on the Narrative Stories

5.5.1 Complexity and Implications of Career-Choice Motivations

The narrative stories of the ten PFPTs revealed "the complex, personal, and situated nature" (Thomson et al., 2012, p. 332) of their decision-making processes in choosing a teacher education program at a university supported by the CGFTE policy. The stories showed that multiple factors could influence pre-service teachers' choices of teaching as a future career.

The six main career-choice motivations that were extracted from the quantitative data also appeared in the narrative data, but the combination of these motivations differed from one individual to another. Moreover, the interviews enriched the meanings of some motivations. For instance, the suggestions from important others, such as parents, friends, and classmates, mainly focused on the practical needs of society and job advantages, with little consideration for the participants' personal interests. Another example of enriched meaning is the understanding of teacher influence. Previous literature commonly suggested that school teachers' influence played a positive role in pre-service teachers' choice of teaching profession (e.g., Fielstra, 1955; Richards, 1960; Su, 1993; Thornton et al., 2002; Younger et al., 2004). However, the interviews revealed that school teachers' influence on pre-service teachers' career choice was not always positive. For instance, Zhen Zhen's narrative story showed that the hardworking, supportive, caring, and responsible Chinese teachers could serve as encouraging role models for students to follow, but their high expectations for their students' future career development often led them to discourage students from following their path to become a teacher.

Several issues related to career education in Chinese high schools were revealed in these narrative stories. Firstly, some students (such as Wen Jing and Xiao Fang) had vague ideas about which university program to choose upon graduation due to a lack of understanding of which profession would best suit them. These students often relied on suggestions from others before making a hasty decision. Secondly, many participants (such as Zhu Min, Bin Bin, and Zhen Zhen) cited fallback careers as their motivation for choosing teaching as a profession. They gave up their original plans due to the "employment situation" (refer to Zhu Min's narrative) or "financial burden" (refer to Bin Bin and Zhen Zhen's narratives) and chose a teacher-training program based on others' suggestions. Unfortunately, these students often lacked motivation in their studies or were forced to study hard due to external pressures. As pre-service teachers in China are mainly recruited from high school graduates, these issues highlight the shortcomings of high school career education. Therefore, it is important to implement career education courses in high schools to enhance students' awareness of the importance of choosing a suitable major/program for their future career and provide them with the necessary knowledge and skills for career development.

Overall, the narrative data complemented the quantitative findings by providing a deeper understanding of the complexity of pre-service teachers' career-choice motivations. It highlights the importance of considering personal, social, and cultural factors in understanding career choices and suggests the need for further research to better understand the decision-making processes of pre-service teachers in different contexts.

5.5.2 How Do Encouraging Policy Terms Impact the Choice of the Teaching Profession

Although these narratives represent the experiences of only a small number of participants, they demonstrate the complexity of how individuals respond to the impacts of different terms of the CGFTE policy on their choice of teaching as a profession. For individuals with poor family backgrounds and extrinsic career-choice motivations, the encouraging policy terms could increase the possibility of choosing teaching as a profession.

Three participants, Da Wu, Bin Bin, and Zhen Zhen, came from rural areas and poverty-stricken families with a monthly family income between 2,000 and 3,000 RMB. Each of them emphasised job advantages as one of their motivations for choosing teaching. The financial and employment priorities from the policy catered to their needs and reassured them that they were correct to become teachers. As Da Wu expressed in his narrative, "I think the stipulations of the policy are really good and appropriate for me. . . . The policy just assures I will be a teacher anyway". Similarly, Bin Bin stated, "My parents do not earn much even though they work hard. I always want to share the financial burden with them. If I join the scheme, I can save a large sum of money for my family".

As the daughter of a poor family, Zhen Zhen admitted, "I personally don't want my parents to spend too much money on my education". When an unexpected car accident happened to her father that resulted in expensive medical expenditures, her whole family was under great stress. When it came to paying university fees, she said, "I just didn't want to ask them [her family] for tuition fees to avoid adding any more pressure on them". Then she learned about the CGFTE policy and knew that undergraduates enrolling in teaching programs at several universities were exempted from paying fees. She was obviously relieved by the benefits provided by the policy and decided to choose a teaching program: "That was great news for me because I can save my parents money if I enrol in it". Therefore, she made up her mind and "chose the major of English education on the application form to University A". The value of becoming a teacher could be increased, and her decision to teach confirmed.

Moreover, the encouraging policy terms seemed to consolidate the choice of teaching for those with a rich family background and intrinsic career-choice motivations. This can be seen from Xiao Fang's story. Xiao Fang came from a relatively richer family (4,000 RMB/month) in a coastal area and had a personal interest in teaching. When it came to choosing a major at university, the impact of the encouraging policy terms seemed to strengthen her choice of a teaching program, as she said in her narrative: "Under the current situation of difficulty in job hunting, the policy term that guaranteed a teaching job for graduates of PFPTs was very attractive. So, I finally took their suggestion and put chemistry education as the major at University A on the application form".

5.5.3 How Do Restrictive Policy Terms Impact the Choice of Teaching Profession?

According to EVT, the restrictive terms of the CGFTE policy are likely to reduce individuals' expectancies for success in the teaching profession, hence decreasing the likelihood that people will choose teaching as their future career. This impact, as the following analyses of qualitative narratives indicated, could be confined to pre-service teachers with extrinsic career-choice motivations (refer to the stories of Wen Jing and Zhu Min). However, for those with intrinsic motivation to teach, these restrictive terms could have no negative impacts on their choice of teaching (refer to Li Wen's story).

Both Wen Jing and Zhu Min had extrinsic motivations to choose teaching as a profession. Influenced by friends' advice and job advantages, Wen Jing chose a teaching program at University A without considering the requirements of a teaching profession. After attending the teacher-training program, she appeared to be unhappy with the restrictive policy terms that required her to commit to teaching long term. In fact, she even considered withdrawing from the program, as her narrative stated, "Sometimes I think that the policy cannot impose restrictions on what I should learn at university because I have the right to break the contract by paying off the contractual penalty if I do not want to become a school teacher after graduation". Additionally, Zhu Min also thought the policy had "a little influence" on her choice of teaching, and she admitted that the restrictive terms "restricted the candidate too much".

Motivated by personal interest in teaching, Li Wen had a completely different story about the influence of the restrictive policy terms on her choice of the teaching profession. It seemed that these restrictive terms did not hinder her from pursuing a teaching profession, as she argued in her narrative that "if you want to become a teacher, it goes without a doubt that the policy will help you a lot". Regarding the term that required a six-year teaching service, she commented, "for a person like me who wants to teach for twenty years or even for the whole life, it is not a problem at all". Similarly, regarding the term that required graduates to return to their home province to provide teaching service, she said, "For me, that is not a problem. I think there is no big difference between my home province Sichuan and other provinces. Furthermore, I like to teach in Sichuan Province, although it is in the southwest of China".

References

Fielstra, C. (1955). An analysis of factors influencing the decision to become a teacher. *The Journal of Educational Research, 48*(9), 659–667.

Richards, R. (1960). Prospective teachers' attitudes towards teaching. *The Journal of Teacher Education, 11*(3), 375–380.

Su, J. Z. X. (1993). The study of the education of educators: A profile of teacher education students. *Journal of Research and Development in Education, 26*(3), 125–132.

Thomson, M. M., Turner, J. E., & Nietfeld, J. L. (2012). A typological approach to investigate the teaching career decision: Motivations and beliefs about teaching of prospective teacher candidates. *Teaching and Teacher Education, 28*(3), 324–335.

Thornton, M., Bricheno, P., & Reid, I. (2002). Students' reasons for wanting to teach in primary school. *Research in Education, 67*(1), 33–43.

Younger, M., Brindley, S., Pedder, D., & Hagger, H. (2004). Starting points: Student teachers' reasons for becoming teachers and their preconceptions of what this will mean. *European Journal of Teacher Education, 27*(3), 245–264.

6 Discussion, Recommendations, Limitations, and Conclusions

Introduction

This chapter discusses two main findings related to the overarching research question of whether the CGFTE policy impacts the career-choice motivations of Chinese pre-service teachers. The quantitative findings indicate that the CGFTE policy has no significant negative impacts on their motivation to choose the teaching profession, but it may potentially undermine their intrinsic career-choice motivation. To analyse these findings, this chapter applies existing literature and proposes theoretical explanations from the perspectives of expectancy–value theory (EVT) and undermining effect of extrinsic reward (UEER) theory. Additionally, specific narrative stories from ten PFPTs are used to support the explanations. Based on the study's issues, recommendations are proposed for improving the funding policy, teacher education, and career education in China. Finally, the chapter analyses the limitations of the present study and suggests future research in this area.

6.1 Discussion of Main Findings

6.1.1 No Significant Negative Impacts on Career-Choice Motivations

The study found no significant differences in five out of six career-choice motivations between policy-funded and self-sponsored pre-service teachers. However, the PFPTs had significantly higher intrinsic motivation than did their self-sponsored counterparts. These results suggest that even though it emphasised extrinsic benefits and restricted professional development, the CGFTE policy did not have a significant negative impact on the career-choice motivation of Chinese pre-service teachers. EVT can theoretically explain this finding, which is empirically supported by the qualitative data.

According to the EVT model (e.g., Eccles, 1987, 2005, 2009; Eccles & Wigfield, 1995; Meece et al., 1990; Wigfield & Eccles, 1992, 2000), individuals' achievement-oriented choices and performance are directly impacted by their expectancies for success in completing a task and the value they attach to the specific task. "Expectancies for success" refer to individuals' beliefs about how well they can perform on an upcoming task currently or in the future. Meanwhile, "task-specific value" refers to the qualities of a task and how those qualities impact individuals' desire to do it. In the CGFTE policy, encouraging terms such as "no-fee education", "guaranteed employment", "professional postgraduate study opportunity", and "availability of school management jobs" could add value for pre-service teachers to choose teaching as a profession. However, restrictive terms such as "six-year teaching service", "one-year rural school service", "no opportunity for academic postgraduate study", and "home-province teaching" could increase the difficulty of teaching and constrain future professional development for some pre-service teachers, thus dampening their expectancies for success in the teaching profession. These two groups of policy terms could potentially have opposite impacts on the choice of a teaching profession of pre-service teachers. These opposite impacts might have counteracted each other for the whole PFPT group, leading to no negative impacts on their career-choice motivation.

The above theoretical explanation is supported by the qualitative narratives of the ten PFPTs. The abstracts from these narratives demonstrate that the impacts of encouraging and restrictive policy terms on the choice of teaching profession are opposite (positive vs. negative) for PFPTs who emphasise the benefits of teaching profession. For those with a high personal interest in teaching, the encouraging terms had positive impacts on their career choice, and the restrictive terms seem to have no negative impacts. When considering the diverse impacts of the two groups of policy terms, the overall result generally supports the theoretical explanation that the impacts of different policy terms may offset or counterbalance for all PFPTs. Thus, it echoes the quantitative result that the CGFTE policy has no negative impact on the career-choice motivation of Chinese pre-service teachers.

The quantitative data analyses revealed that there were no significant differences between the PFPTs and their self-sponsored counterparts in the ratings for five of the career-choice motivations: teacher influence, job advantages (extrinsic motivation), social value (altruistic motivation), others' suggestions, and fallback career. That is, the CGFTE policy has no significant impact on these five motivations for pre-service teachers to choose teaching as a profession. Therefore, the encouraging terms of the CGFTE policy, such as "no-fee teacher education", "guaranteed employment", "professional postgraduate study opportunity", and "availability of school management posts", do not significantly attract more students who emphasise job advantages of the teaching profession or choose teaching as a fallback career into policy-funded teacher-training programs. This finding is encouraging, as previous studies (e.g., Bruinsma & Jansen, 2010; Sinclair et al., 2006) suggest that extrinsic career choice motivation and choosing teaching as a fallback career are related to negative teaching experiences and teacher attrition. Without

Discussion, Recommendation, Limitation, and Conclusion 89

such maladaptive motivations, PFPTs are more likely to become in-service teachers who will teach for a long period, thereby achieving the aim of the CGFTE policy to build a stable teaching force.

It was found that the only type of career-choice motivation that the PFPTs rated significantly higher than their self-sponsored counterparts was personal interest, an intrinsic motivation. Further analysis revealed that the CGFTE policy had a significant effect on the personal interest of Chinese pre-service teachers independent of their demographic background, reflecting that the CGFTE policy attracts students with a significantly higher personal interest in teaching to teacher-training programs. As previous researchers established (e.g., Canrinus & Fokkens-Bruinsma, 2014; Hauge et al., 1997; Malmberg, 2006), intrinsic career-choice motives are positively related to pre-service teachers' future professional development, such as job satisfaction, retention, and commitment to teaching. Moreover, researchers (e.g., Bruinsma & Jansen, 2010) have shown that intrinsic motivation is adaptive and positively related to the quality of teacher-training programs and classroom teaching experience. Therefore, the results of the present study suggest that PFPTs, despite facing many restrictions imposed by the policy, are likely to become high-quality teachers who will stay in the profession for a longer period than their self-funded counterparts. This, in turn, indicates that the goals of the CGFTE policy, such as building a group of high-quality teachers willing to teach for six years, can be achieved.

6.1.2 Possible Undermining Impacts on Intrinsic Career-Choice Motivation

As the quantitative analyses showed, overall, the PFPTs had significantly higher intrinsic career-choice motivation than their self-funded counterparts. However, a further comparison between first-year and final-year participants demonstrated that, during the pre-service teacher education program at universities, intrinsic career-choice motivation declined among the PFPTs but increased among the SSPTs. Although the difference in intrinsic motivation between first-year and final-year students did not reach statistical significance, the divergent trends of intrinsic motivation between policy-funded and self-funded pre-service teachers suggest a potential influence from the CGFTE policy. This section explores this possibility by analysing it through the lens of UEER theory.

UEER theory describes the phenomenon where people who are offered extrinsic rewards for a task lose some of their initial intrinsic motivation to perform that task (Graham & Weiner, 2012). The theory also suggests that introducing extrinsic rewards for a task or activity that is initially conducted without such rewards reduces interest in the activity once the rewards are no longer available. This is known as the "over-justification effect" (Akin-Little & Little, 2004; Lepper et al., 1973). According to UEER theory, several conditions must be met for the phenomenon to occur, including tangible, expected, and non-contingent rewards, as well as high initial interest in the task (Graham & Weiner, 2012). The encouraging terms of the CGFTE policy, such as tuition-free university education, a guaranteed teaching job, a professional postgraduate study opportunity, and the availability of school management positions, appear to meet these conditions. These rewards are tangible extrinsic rewards rather than symbolic ones, and they are not contingent on academic achievement during university study. Therefore, UEER theory suggests that the encouraging terms of the CGFTE policy may function as extrinsic rewards that reduce the intrinsic motivation of pre-service teachers to choose teaching as a profession.

The present study's results suggest a potential undermining effect of the encouraging policy terms on the intrinsic career-choice motivation of PFPTs. Whereas the PFPTs as a whole had significantly higher intrinsic career-choice motivation than their self-funded counterparts, the last-year policy-funded students had lower intrinsic motivation than their first-year counterparts. In contrast, the last-year SSPTs had slightly higher intrinsic motivation than their first-year counterparts. As demonstrated by the results of the self-funded pre-service teachers, the four-year teacher training likely increases pre-service teachers' personal interest in the teaching profession. However, according to UEER theory, the withdrawal of some extrinsic rewards in the CGFTE policy for last-year PFPTs, such as the end of free teacher training and the fulfilment of guaranteed employment for policy-funded graduates, would decrease their intrinsic motivation to choose teaching as a profession.

The potential undermining effect of the CGFTE policy on pre-service teachers' intrinsic career-choice motivation, as discussed above, should be approached with caution for two reasons. Firstly, while graphical displays demonstrated a divergent trend in intrinsic motivation between policy-funded and self-funded pre-service teachers during teacher training, statistical results indicated that the difference in intrinsic career-choice motivation between first-year and last-year PFPTs was not statistically significant at the .05 level. Additionally, because the present research was not longitudinal, the first-year and last-year pre-service teachers are different participants, and other factors may have influenced their differences in intrinsic motivation. Therefore, longitudinal studies are needed to examine changes in intrinsic career-choice motivation among the same group of PFPTs from the beginning of teacher training to program completion to determine whether the CGFTE policy has an undermining effect on their intrinsic motivation to choose teaching as a profession.

6.2 Recommendations

The findings of the present study and the discussions above reveal several issues related to the CGFTE policy, teacher education, and career education in China. To address these issues, it is recommended to improve the CGFTE policy by changing some policy terms and strengthening supportive measures for carrying out the policy; reforming teacher education in China in the areas of recruiting, training, and evaluating pre-service teachers at university; and emphasising the importance of career education in high schools in China.

6.2.1 Improving the Central Government-Funded Teacher Education Policy

The CGFTE policy aims to cultivate a high-quality and stable teaching force willing to serve in rural schools for one year, offering benefits such as tuition-free education, free accommodation, and an allowance for living costs. However, debates have arisen about the policy's negative impact on pre-service teachers' motivation to choose teaching (e.g., Chen, 2013; Di et al., 2022; Wu & Liu, 2008). Whereas the present study did not find an overall negative impact, the decline in intrinsic career-choice motivation among PFPTs during teacher training suggests that some of the policy terms may have potential undermining effects.

Further analyses revealed that the PFPTs were most dissatisfied with two terms in the CGFTE policy: "no opportunity for academic postgraduate study" and "mandatory return to home province for teaching". Policy-funded students who comply with these terms and begin long-term teaching services immediately after graduation might be deprived of the opportunity to pursue further academic education, and their future career development might be limited. The narrative stories revealed that these terms could reduce the likelihood of choosing education programs and lead to relatively low and declining study engagement among students with extrinsic motivation to teach. Therefore, it is recommended to explore potential modifications of these policy terms, as outlined below, to reduce their potential undermining effects.

Firstly, some PFPTs should be allowed to take exams for academic postgraduate study. For those who pass the exams, their teaching services could be postponed until they complete their postgraduate studies. This could ensure the provision of teaching services while also guaranteeing the educational rights of those who wish to further their studies and enhance the quality of their teaching services. Secondly, further studies should be conducted to determine whether graduates from policy-funded teacher education programs should be able to negotiate where they teach. With no limitation to home-province teaching, high-quality graduates can teach in provinces where teachers are in scarcity, which could help improve the equal distribution of high-quality teaching force across different provinces.

Additionally, the supportive measures for implementing the CGFTE policy need to be improved. Firstly, the importance of the policy should be widely publicised in society, and the details of the policy terms should be explained carefully to high school graduates before they complete university application forms. This will ensure that parents and students fully understand the benefits and obligations they will have if they choose the policy-funded programs and thereby reduce the likelihood of choosing teaching as a fallback career or feeling regretful during teacher training. Secondly, a sound mechanism should be established for policy-funded students to withdraw from the policy-funded teacher-training programs. This can help select high-quality teaching candidates by filtering out those who have low personal interest in the teaching profession or low study engagement in training programs. Lastly, the salary and social status of teachers need to be raised, and teaching conditions in rural schools should be improved. When teachers are well rewarded and highly respected in society, teaching as a profession will become more popular to pursue, and improving the teaching conditions of poor schools can attract high-quality teachers to stay for long-term teaching. Improving the CGFTE policy and its supportive measures simultaneously is more likely to achieve the goal of retaining qualified teachers in schools (Shang, 2017).

6.2.2 Reforming Teacher Education at Universities

The primary criterion for recruiting candidates into teacher-education programs at universities in China is currently their scores on the selective NCEE, which are supposed to represent their academic performance. However, the low ranking of intrinsic career-choice motivation among Chinese pre-service teachers demonstrated in the current study could be partly due to the lack of examination of candidates' motivation to choose teaching as their future profession. Furthermore, the decline of personal interest in becoming a teacher among PFPTs during the four-year teacher training at universities implementing the CGFTE policy suggest the need to improve teacher-training curriculum design and assessment of the universities for pre-service teachers.

To address these issues, it is recommended to interview pre-service teachers at each teacher-training university to establish teaching motivation profiles of the student bodies that should then be updated annually. This could provide useful information for different stakeholders in teacher education (Liu, 2010). Teacher educators can better understand and support pre-service teachers, educational researchers can analyse the relationship between pre-service teachers' career-choice motivation and other related factors, and university leaders and policymakers can implement proper plans and policies on pre-service teacher recruitment and preparation, and design high-quality teacher-education programs according to the data in the profiles.

To effectively recruit pre-service teacher candidates into teacher-training programs, it is recommended that schools adopt admission interviews. In western countries, three measures are usually taken for recruiting new teachers, credential test scores, surveys, and interviews. However, the sequence for implementing them usually leads to different results (Kennedy, 2008). In China, it is suggested that pre-service teacher candidates undergo admission interviews before their NCEE scores are checked. During the interviews, their attitudes towards teaching should be examined, and their career-choice motivation profiles should be consulted. Only those who meet all the criteria of teaching attitude, career-choice motivation, and exam scores should be recruited into teacher-training programs.

Lastly, it is recommended that the curricula and evaluation systems in teacher-training universities be reformed. The curricula should focus more on practical teaching skills than educational theories, and the evaluation criteria should be diversified to not only test knowledge but also assess teaching skills, affection, and attitudes of pre-service teachers.

6.2.3 Strengthening Career Education in High Schools

Contrary to most research findings in western contexts where intrinsic motivation was frequently found to be the most influential factor, Chinese pre-service teachers, as demonstrated in the results of this study, ranked intrinsic motivation as the fourth most important factor among their six reasons for choosing a teaching profession. Interviews with Chinese pre-service teachers also showed that their choice of teaching was often influenced by extrinsic factors, such as parents' suggestions and the benefits of the CGFTE policy. Some even changed their original plans at the last moment just for the benefits of the teaching profession and the policy. These problems, to a large degree, can be attributed to the shortage of career education in high schools in China.

In most schools on the Chinese mainland, counselling services for students about their future career development have rarely been provided (Liu, 2010). The reasons behind this may be diverse, but the major attribution should be the pervasive effects of the so-called examination-oriented education on school teaching, student learning, and class management. Almost all school teachers and leaders mainly focus their time and energy on improving students' academic achievement and their scores on exams, which has resulted in the neglect of students' important aspect of future career development.

Without career counselling, high school graduates may face challenges in making career plans. They may hesitate when making decisions about which university major to study, as their decisions are often related to their future careers. This problem could become even more severe for PFPTs because, upon graduation from high school, they need to sign a contract with the local government promising to teach for six years after graduation from the university.

Therefore, it is recommended that Chinese high schools emphasise career counselling. With scientific guidance and orientation courses, high school students can be equipped with knowledge about their own personalities as well as the features of different careers, which can help them understand their personal interests and develop skills suitable for specific careers. In this way, upon graduation from high school, they will be more confident and rational in choosing a university major, and their choice of education programs will more likely be based on personal interest.

6.3 Limitations and Future Studies

The present study is significant in exploring the impacts of the CGFTE policy on the career-choice motivations of Chinese pre-service teachers. However, due to the restriction of research resources, there are limitations in the study regarding the representativeness of participants, the survey instruments and techniques applied, and the research approach followed. Future studies are recommended to overcome these limitations and contribute more knowledge to this field.

This study surveyed participants in 2013 from three universities, one implementing the CGFTE policy and the other two not. The relevance of these data persists due to the essentially unchanged CGFTE policy throughout the past decade. However, future studies are expected to provide new and updated data. Although the home regions of these participants covered most provinces of China, all three universities were located in southwest and central China, where the economic development levels are generally lower than the northeast and coastal regions of the country. It is uncertain whether the locations of teacher-training universities could influence the career-choice motivations of Chinese pre-service teachers, but future studies involving universities from a wider range of areas across China will increase the representativeness of findings.

For each university in the present study, only first-year and last-year pre-service teachers were surveyed to compare their career-choice motivations. However, without sampling second-year and third-year students, the entire picture of changes during the four-year teacher training at the university cannot be revealed. Therefore, future studies are suggested to investigate pre-service teachers from all four years of study to describe the changing trend during teacher training. The results will provide useful information for designing effective curricula for students in each year of study and for reforming instruction skills for training pre-service teachers.

This study applied a qualitative approach of online audio interviews after the quantitative explorations in order to have a fuller understanding of the quantitative findings. However, only ten policy-funded students participated in the interviews; the small number of interviewees could limit the representativeness and reliability of their narrative stories. Moreover, although the online audio interviews allowed interviewees to express their real inner voices by hiding their images from the researcher, some important information in the interviews may have been lost as the researcher was unable to observe their facial expressions. Therefore, future studies are suggested to use multiple qualitative study methods, such as face-to-face interviews, group discussions, and classroom observations, to gather information and voices from more pre-service teachers, as well as their parents, teacher educators, university leaders, and policymakers.

The current study used both quantitative and qualitative approaches to explore the impacts of the CGFTE policy on Chinese pre-service teachers' initial motivations to choose the teaching profession. As it was not a longitudinal study, the future career development of these pre-service teachers could not be followed up. Similar to existing literature in the research field of teacher motivation (e.g., Richardson & Watt, 2010, 2014), future longitudinal studies are recommended for exploring the relationships between pre-service teachers' career-choice motivations and their future career development and for tracking the same group of PFPTs throughout a course of university education to examine whether the policy aims are achieved or not in the long run.

6.4 Conclusion

Overall, the CGFTE policy has no significant negative impacts on the career-choice motivations of Chinese pre-service teachers. This finding is interesting as it indicates that the policy terms, which emphasise extrinsic benefits of the teaching profession and constrict the professional development of pre-service teachers, turn out to have no significant side effects on pre-service teachers' motivation to choose teaching as a profession during teacher training. This finding, together with the relatively high intrinsic career-choice motivation of PFPTs, suggests that the aim of the CGFTE policy – to build a high-quality and stable teaching force – is likely to be achieved. However, during teacher training, PFPTs appear to experience a decline in their intrinsic career-choice motivation. This indicates the need to reform the CGFTE policy, teacher education, and high school career education in China. Future longitudinal studies are recommended that examine the impacts of the CGFTE policy on PFPTs' professional development and evaluate the effectiveness of the policy in achieving its goals.

The main finding of this study seems to be supported by EVT, which argues that an individual's expectancy for success in completing a task and the task-specific value they perceive directly predict their achievement-related choice and performance. The restrictive terms of the CGFTE policy could dampen some PFPTs' expectancy for success in the teaching profession, while the encouraging terms are likely to add extra value to the profession. As shown in the narrative stories, these different terms in the CGFTE policy could exert opposite impacts on the choice of teaching for different PFPTs. Therefore, for the whole PFPT population, these opposite impacts could counteract each other and thus concur with the quantitative finding that the CGFTE policy has no negative impacts on their motivation to choose teaching as a profession.

Meanwhile, the decline in intrinsic career-choice motivation for PFPTs could be supported by UEER theory. The encouraging policy terms, such as "tuition-free teacher education", "guaranteed teaching job", and "opportunity for professional postgraduate study", seem to meet the criteria of extrinsic rewards in the theory and thus could produce undermining effects on pre-service teachers' intrinsic motivation to choose teaching as a profession. However, because the decline in intrinsic motivation did not reach statistical significance, potential undermining effects of these encouraging policy terms need to be further examined in future studies.

Additionally, the findings reported in this study describe some characteristics of Chinese pre-service teachers. They are predominantly female, young, and Han majority and many are from rural-area families with low incomes. Six motivations for choosing teaching as a career were identified: in decreasing order of importance, teacher influence, job advantages (extrinsic motivation), social value (altruistic motivation), personal interest (intrinsic motivation), other's suggestion, and fallback career. The narrative stories illustrate that the six career-choice motivations are multifaceted and interrelated, often intertwined with each other in complex ways, revealing their rich and nuanced meanings. These findings provide a framework to better inform policymakers and universities in harnessing the existing career-choice motivations of pre-service teachers.

Findings from this study and the theorisation of these findings are situation specific, but they can still be considered in international contexts outside of China. It would be interesting to explore whether the reduced CCM scale or a similar instrument could be useful in selecting high-quality candidates for teacher education programs in different contexts. In reality, other countries utilise various forms of selective funding to attract and retain teachers in rural areas (e.g., Monk, 2007; Sclafani, 2010), from minority groups (e.g., Kearney-Gissendaner, 2013; Phillion et al., 2011), or with specific subject expertise (e.g., Drew, 2011; Freeman et al., 2015). Although this study is localised in China, it suggests that such incentives may have both desirable and undesirable results. Before countries widely adopt such policies, it would be useful to research which elements are effective in motivating and retaining teachers and which ones may undermine the intentions of such policies.

References

Akin-Little, K. A., & Little, S. G. (2004). Re-examining the overjustification effect. *Journal of Behavioral Education*, *13*(3), 179–192.
Bruinsma, M., & Jansen, E. (2010). Is the motivation to become a teacher related to pre-service teachers' intentions to remain in the profession? *European Journal of Teacher Education*, *33*(2), 185–200.
Canrinus, E. T., & Fokkens-Bruinsma, M. (2014). Changes in student teachers' motives and the meaning of teacher education program quality. *European Journal of Teacher Education*, *37*(3), 262–278.
Chen, Y.-G. (2013). Daxuesheng weilai quxiang, zhuanye rentong yu xuexi touru de guanxi [The relationship between future orientation, study engagement and professional identity of college students]. *Si Chuan Wen Li Xue Yuan Xue Bao*, *23*(2), 91–95.
Di, Y., Feng, S., & Tan, Y. (2022). Jiyu jiaoxue zhiliang de gongfei shifan jiaoyu zhengce yanjiu [Research on the policy-funded normal students' education from the perspective of teaching quality]. *Jiao Yu Ke Xue*, *38*(1), 49–56.

Drew, D. E. (2011). *STEM the tide: Reforming science, technology, engineering, and math education in America.* The Johns Hopkins University Press.

Eccles, J. S. (1987). Gender roles and women's achievement-related decisions. *Psychology of Women Quarterly, 11*(2), 135–171.

Eccles, J. S. (2005). Subjective task value and the Eccles et al. model of achievement-related choice. In A. J. Elliot & C. S. Dweck (Eds.), *Handbook of competence and motivation.* Guilford.

Eccles, J. S. (2009). Who am I and what am I going to do with my life? Personal and collective identities as motivators of action. *Educational Psychologist, 44*(2), 78–89.

Eccles, J. S., & Wigfield, A. (1995). In the mind of the actor: The structure of adolescents' achievement task values and expectancy-related beliefs. *Personality and Social Psychology Bulletin, 21*(3), 215–225.

Freeman, B., Marginson, S., & Tytler, R. (Eds.). (2015). *The age of STEM: Educational policy and practice across the world in science, technology, engineering and mathematics.* Routledge.

Graham, S., & Weiner, B. (2012). Motivation: Past, present, and future. In K. R. Harris, S. Graham, T. Urdan, C. B. McCormick, G. M. Sinatra, & J. Sweller (Eds.), *APA educational psychology handbook, Vol 1: Theories, constructs, and critical issues.* American Psychological Association.

Hauge, T., Björkqvist, O., Hansén, S.-E., Carlgren, I., & Bergem, T. (1997). Research on teachers and teacher education in Scandinavia: A retrospective review. *Scandinavian Journal of Educational Research, 41*(3), 433–458.

Kearney-Gissendaner, J. E. (2013). *Minority teacher recruitment and retention strategies.* Routledge.

Kennedy, M. M. (2008). Sorting out teacher quality. *The Phi Delta Kappan, 90*(1), 59–63.

Lepper, M. R., Greene, D., & Nisbett, R. E. (1973). Understanding children's intrinsic interest with extrinsic reward: A test of the "overjustification" hypothesis. *Journal of Personality and Social Psychology, 28*(1).

Liu, P. (2010). Examining perspectives of entry-level teacher candidates: A comparative study. *Australian Journal of Teacher Education, 35*(5), 56–78.

Malmberg, L.-E. (2006). Goal-orientation and teacher motivation among teacher applicants and student teachers. *Teaching and Teacher Education, 22*(1), 58–76.

Meece, J. L., Wigfield, A., & Eccles, J. S. (1990). Predictors of math anxiety and its influence on young adolescents' course enrollment intentions and performance in mathematics. *Journal of Educational Psychology, 82*(1), 60.

Monk, D. H. (2007). Recruiting and retaining high-quality teachers in rural areas. *The Future of Children, 17*(1), 155–174.

Phillion, J., Hue, M. T., & Wang, Y. (Eds.). (2011). *Minority students in East Asia: Government policies, school practices, and teacher responses.* Routledge.

Richardson, P. W., & Watt, H. M. G. (2010). Current and future directions in teacher motivation research. In T. C. Urdan & S. A. Karabenick (Eds.), *The decade ahead: Applications and contexts of motivation and achievement (Advances in motivation and achievement, Vol. 16)* (pp. 139–173). Emerald Group Publishing Limited.

Richardson, P. W., & Watt, H. M. G. (2014). Why people choose teaching as a career: An expectancy-value approach to understanding teacher motivation. In P. W. Richardson, S. A. Karabenick, & H. M. G. Watt (Eds.), *Teacher motivation: Theory and practice* (pp. 3–19). Routledge.

Sclafani, S. (2010). Teacher compensation around the globe. *The Phi Delta Kappan, 91*(8), 38–43.

Shang, Y. (2017). Mianfei shifansheng jiuye zhengce shishi 10 zhounian zhuizong yanjiu – – yi dongbei shifan daxue wujie mianfei shifansheng weili [The follow-up study of the implementation of the employment policy of free normal university students on the 10th anniversary: A case study of graduates from the northeast normal university in five consecutive years]. *Jiao Yu Yan Jiu, 455*(12), 141–146.

Sinclair, C., Dowson, M., & McInerney, D. M. (2006). Motivations to teach: Psychometric perspectives across the first semester of teacher education. *Teachers College Record, 108*(6), 1132–1154.

Wigfield, A., & Eccles, J. S. (1992). The development of achievement task values: A theoretical analysis. *Developmental Review, 12*(3), 265–310.

Wigfield, A., & Eccles, J. S. (2000). Expectancy-value theory of achievement motivation. *Contemporary Educational Psychology, 25*(1), 68–68.

Wu, Z.-M., & Liu, F. (2008). Mianfei shifansheng jiaoyu zhengce chuyi [On the policy of free education for undergraduates in normal universities]. *Hang Zhou Shi Fan Da Xue Xue Bao (She Hui Ke Xue Ban), 6*.

Appendices

Appendix 1

Part A (Chinese and English Translation) of the Survey

第一部分：个人基本情况（请在相应选项代码上划"√" 或在横线上填写信息）

A1. 性别： （1）男 （2）女
A2. 民族： （1）汉族 （2）少数民族
A3. 生源地： （1）农村 （2）城镇
A4. 年级： （1）大一 （2）大四
A5. 您来自_____省/市，年龄_____岁，家庭收入大约为_____元/月
A6. 您的高考分数为____分，属于___科（文、理或综合）___本（一、二或三），该分数超过当年相应科类、批次的省控制分数线___分，现就读于_____大学/学院。
A7. 大学本科毕业后，您任教的学校最可能为：
（1）幼儿园 （2）小学 （3）初中 （4）高中 （5）大学 （6）不确定
A8. 大学本科毕业后，您任教的科目最可能为：
（1）语文 （2）数学 （3）外语 （4）政治 （5）历史 （6）地理 （7）物理 （8）化学 （9）生物 （10）艺体类 （11）其他科类 （12）不确定
注：如果您愿意参加本研究的后续访谈，请填写你的联系方式：
QQ号：_____ 电子邮箱：_____

Part A: Basic Information (Please Tick '√' and Fill in the Gaps)

A1. Gender: (1) Male   (2) Female
A2. Ethnicity: (1) Han People   (2) Ethnic Minorities
A3. Hometown: (1) Rural Area   (2) Urban Area
A4. Year of Study: (1) First Year   (2) Fourth (Last) Year

A5. I come from ___ Province; I am ___ years old; my family income is around ___ RMB per month.

A6. My score of the National College Entrance Examination was ___, which belonged to ___ discipline (Arts, Science or Combined) ___ Level (First, Second or Third). My scores surpassed the National College Cut-off Score by ___ points, and now I am studying at ___ University.

A7. After graduation from the university, which of the following educational institutions will you probably go to teach?

(1) Kindergarten (2) Primary School (3) Junior High School (4) Senior High School (5) University (6) I am not sure

A8. After graduation from the university, which of the following subjects will you probably go to teach?

(1) Chinese (2) Math (3) Foreign language (4) Politics (5) History (6) Geography (7) Physics (8) Chemistry (9) Biology (10) Arts and PE (11) Other subjects (12) I am not sure

Note: If you would like to participate in our follow-up interviews, please write down your contact information here: QQ Account_____; Email Address: _____.

Appendix 2

Part B of the Factors Influencing Teaching Choice Scale (FIT-Choice Scale): Sample Items (English and Chinese Translations)

Part B: Career-Choice Motivation (The CCM Scale)
第二部分：职业选择的动机 (职业选择动机问卷)

Item stem: "I chose to become a teacher because . . ." 我选择成为教师，因为......

Anchor: 1 (not at all important) to 7 (extremely important) 1(完全不重要)至7(极为重要)

Higher-Order Factor	Factor	Sam. Item#	Original English	Chinese Translation
N/A	Ability	B5	I have the qualities of a good teacher	我有当一名好老师的品质
N/A	Intrinsic career value	B1	I am interested in teaching	我对教书感兴趣
N/A	Fallback career	B10	I was unsure of what career I wanted	我还没有确定我以后的职业
Personal utility value	Job security	B13	Teaching will offer a steady career path	教书是个稳定的职业
	Time for family	B2	Part-time teaching could allow more family time	每天部分时间上课，能让教师有较多时间与家人相处
	Job transferability	B8	Teaching will be a useful job for me to have when travelling	教书能使我有机会在其他城市或国家工作
Social utility value	Shape future of children/adolescents	B9	Teaching will allow me to shape child/adolescent values	教书能让我有机会帮助青少年树立正确价值观

(Continued)

Higher-Order Factor	Factor	Sam. Item#	Original English	Chinese Translation
	Enhance social equity	B28	Teaching will allow me to raise the ambitions of underprivileged youth	教书可以让我帮助弱势青少年建立远大的理想
	Make social contribution	B6	Teaching allows me to provide a service to society	教学可以让我服务于社会
	Work with children/adolescents	B12	I want a job that involves working with children/adolescents	我喜欢与小孩及青少年有接触的工作
N/A	Prior teaching and learning experience	B15	I have had inspirational teachers	我曾经有过能鼓动人心的老师
N/A	Social influences	B3	My friends think I should become a teacher	我的朋友认为我应该当老师

Note: The full 38 items of Part B of the FIT-Choice Scale were developed and validated by Watt and Richardson (2007). The Chinese version was originally translated by Lin et al. (2012) and adapted for the present study.

Appendix 3
Interview Outline (Chinese and English Translation)

Items#	Chinese	English Translation
A	请介绍一下您自己，包括你的兴趣和专业。	Please introduce yourself, including your interests and university major.
B	为什么选择将来做中小学教师？	Why did you choose to become a school teacher in the future?
C	高中毕业时，你是怎样做出决定，选择大学师范专业的？	When you graduated from high school, how did you make the decision to choose a university major in education?
D	在"师范生公费教育政策"中，（1）哪些规定让您最满意？为什么？（2）哪些规定让您最不满意？为什么？	Which terms in the Central Government-Funded Teacher Education (CGFTE) policy do you find most satisfying? Why? Which terms do you find least satisfying? Why?
	可能的跟进问题：	Possible follow-up questions:
a	你觉得"从事中小学教师职业六年"怎么样？为什么？	What do you think of "six years of school teaching"? Why?
b	"到农村从事一年中小学教学"，你觉得怎么样？为什么？	What do you think of "teaching in a rural area school for one year"? Why?
c	你觉得"回生源所在省份从教"怎么样？为什么？	What do you think of "teaching in your home province after graduation"? Why?
d	毕业后你想读全日制硕士研究生吗？（1）如果想，你怎样看待失去攻读全日制硕士的机会？（2）如果不想，为什么？你将来的计划是怎样的呢？	Do you want to pursue a full-time master's degree after graduation? (1) If so, how do you feel about missing the opportunity to pursue a full-time master's degree? (2) If not, why not? What are your future plans?
E	总体而言，对"师范生公费教育政策"，您有什么看法？	Overall, what are your thoughts on the CGFTE policy?

Appendix 4
Changes to the Chinese Translations of Part B of the FIT-Choice Scale

Item	Original (or adapted) English	Original Chinese Translation	Chinese translated in present study	Reasons for making changes
B2	Part-time teaching could allow more family time.	当兼职教师让我有比较多的时间跟家人相处。	每天部分时间上课，能让教师有较多时间与家人相处。	In this study, the participants are bound by the CGFTE policy, which requires them to become full-time teachers. Therefore, item B2 was revised to indicate "teaching during a portion of the day" to align with the specific context.
B8	Teaching will be a useful job for me to have when travelling.	教书能使我机会在其他城市或国家工作。	教书能使我有机会在其他城市或国家工作。	The original sentence lacks a verb in Chinese.
B9	Teaching will allow me to shape child/adolescent values	教书能让我有机会帮助青少年树立价值观。	教书能让我有机会帮助青少年树立正确价值观。	Align the translation of Chinese with Chinese idiomatic expressions.
B27	I was not accepted into my first-choice career	我没能做到我最想要做到的工作。	我没能做到我最想要做到的职业。	Ensure consistency in the Chinese translation of the term "career".

Item	Original (or adapted) English	Original Chinese Translation	Chinese translated in present study	Reasons for making changes
B32	People I've worked with think I should become a teacher	和我一起**工作的同事**觉得我应该当老师。	和我一起**学习的同学**觉得我应该当老师。	The participants in this study are pre-service teachers, who are university students without colleagues in a professional work setting.
B37	Teaching will allow me to have an impact on children/ adolescents	教书可以让我机会对青少年产生影响。	教书可以让我**有**机会对青少年产生影响。	The original sentence lacks a verb in Chinese.

Note: The bold words indicate changes made by the current study in the Chinese translation.

Index

Note: Page numbers in *italics* indicate a figure and page numbers in **bold** indicate a table on the corresponding page. Page numbers followed by "n" with numbers refer to notes.

academic postgraduate study *see* CGFTE policy restrictive terms
altruistic motivation: Chinese and Hong Kong SAR pre-service teachers' 23; love for children 23; social value 47, 55, 57–59, 63, 88, 96; socio-cultural contexts 20
American high school students, career motivation 18
American pre-service teachers, career motivation: compared to Chinese pre-service teachers 22–23; compared to Cypress pre-service teachers 20; culture defining 24; intrinsic motivation 18, 20, 22; most popular motivation 22; perception of teaching 22; role of teachers 22; satisfaction with teaching as a career choice 23
anti-image correlation values 52, 53
Atputhasamy, L. 19
"attainment value" 10; *see also* Expectancy–Value Theory (EVT)
attractors 17, 23–24
Australian pre-service teachers, career motivation: gender differences 27; high status 28; self evaluation (characteristics and abilities) 18

Bartlett's test of sphericity 52, 53
Bin Bin's story 67, 78–80, 83, 84; *see also* PFPTs narrative stories, ten cases
Brookhart, S. M 25
Bruinsma, M 89

Cambria, J. 10
Canrinus, E. T 19
career-choice motivation scale (CCM Scale) 41, 52; complexity and implications of 83–84; component analysis, screen test for 55; component factors, extraction of 54; *see also* FIT-Choice Scale
Central Government Annual Report (2007) 4
Central Government-Funded Teacher Education (CGFTE) policy 1; contents 5–7; educational equality 4; encouraging terms 84–85, 90; funded pre-service teachers 30–31; goals 4–5; guaranteed employment 88; impacts on career-choice motivation 58–63; implementation contexts for 3–4; potential undermining effect of 90; pre-service teachers 5, 8–9; research themes and trends 29–30; restrictive terms 7–8, 85–86; teacher-education programs 5
CGFTE *see* Central Government-Funded Teacher Education (CGFTE) policy
CGFTE policy encouraging terms 7, 7, 12, 88, 90, 95
CGFTE policy restrictive terms 7, 7, 8, 85, 88, 95
Chinese pre-service teachers: career choice motivation, funded of 8–9;

and CGFTE policy 3–7; and EVT 10–11; definition 9; family background 27; history of free education 1–3; literature review 20–23; study rationale 1; undermining effects of extrinsic reward theory 11–12; *see also* altruistic motivation; extrinsic motivation; intrinsic motivation
Chongqing Municipality 43, 49
classroom observations 94
consent form 42, 43, 44
continuation attractors 24
correlation matrix 52, 53
"cost" 10; *see also* Expectancy–Value Theory (EVT) model
Cronbach's alpha 56, 57
Cultural Revolution (1966–1976) 21

Da Wu's story 67, 69–71, 84; *see also* PFPTs narrative stories, ten cases
descriptive statistics analysis 48
Doliopoulou, E. 19
Dutch pre-service teachers, career motivation 19

"early and affective decisions" (facilitator) 24
Eccles, J. S 10
eigenvalues 53
English teacher-education programs 21
"entry under constraint" (facilitator) 24
encouraging terms *see* CGFTE policy encouraging terms
Evans, H. 19
examination-oriented education 93
"expectancies for success" 10–11, 88; *see also* Expectancy–Value Theory (EVT)
Expectancy–Value Theory (EVT) 1, 10–11, 87, 95
expectation maximisation (EM) approach 48
exploratory factor analysis 52
extrinsic motivation: developing countries students 20; Jamaican pre-service teachers 20; job advantages 47, 55, 57, 57–58, 59, 63, 88; teacher influence 47, 57–58, 88
extrinsic value identity (three-dimensional model) 31

face-to-face interviews 94
facilitators 17, 23–24
factor analysis 25, 52–54
factor-loading matrix 55, 57
factor pattern matrix 54
factors influencing teaching choice scale (FIT-Choice Scale) *see* FIT-Choice scale
female teachers 26, 80
FIT-Choice scale 19, 20, 32, 40, 41, 42, 57, 96
Freeman, D. J. 25
Fokkens-Bruinsma, M. 19
future studies 94–95

Goh, K. C. 19
government-funded teacher-education programs 5, 27
government-funded teacher-training programs 8, 12, 30
Graham, S. 9, 10
group discussions 94

high score group 51, 59
"home-province teaching" 88; *see also* CGFTE policy encouraging terms
Hunan Province 43, 49

Imperial University Teacher College 2
independent-samples t tests 47, 58, 63
information sheet 42, 43, 44
in-service teachers 23, 32, 89
interpersonal attractors 23–24
intrinsic career-choice motivation: and CGFTE policy terms 95; decline during teacher training of PFPTs 63–64, 95; effect of CGFTE 47; fourth most important factor 93; high, of PFPTs 95; influence of gender 60; no overall negative impact of CGFTE on 91; potential undermining impact on of PFPTs' 87, 89–90; teacher education reform 92
intrinsic motivation: CGFTE policy and demographic variables 58–59; CGFTE policy fail 47; CGFTE policy impacts on PFPTs 58–63; Chinese pre-service teachers 22; decline during teacher training of PFPTs 47; and female pre-service teachers 27; and gender 61;

higher in CGFTE 47; Hong Kong SAR pre-service teachers 21; impact of restrictive policy terms on 85–86; improving career education in high schools 93; Irish pre-service teachers 19; quantitative findings 63–64; potential undermining impact on, of PFPTs' 87, 89–90; Singaporean pre-service teachers 19; study conclusion on 96; theory of UEER 11–12;
intrinsic value (interest) 10, 18, 19, 20, 22, 27
intrinsic value identity 31
Irish pre-service teachers 19

Jamaican pre-service teachers, career motivation 20
Jansen, E. 89
job security (motivator) 18, 21, 23, 54

kindergarten teacher 19, 66, 78
König, J. 19

Levene's tests 59; see also univariate tests
Likert-type (1 to 7) self-reported scale 41
literature review: CGFTE Policy, studies on 29–31; summary of 31–32; teachers' career-choice motivations 17–29
Li, L. 21
Lin, E. 22
Li Wen's story 66–69, 85; see also PFPTs narrative stories, ten cases
Lortie, D. C. 23–25
Lortie's framework 24; see also motivational factors
Lovett, S. 18

Macau SAR pre-service teachers, career motivation 21
male teachers 26, 80
material benefits attractors 24
measures of sampling adequacy (MSA) 52
medium score group 51
Meng Meng's story 66, 67, 82–83; see also PFPTs narrative stories, ten cases
metric variables 48

"middling" value 52
Ming Mei's story 66, 67, 72–73; see also PFPTs narrative stories, ten cases
Ministry of Education of China 4
missing data 47–48
mixed-methods research design: ethical considerations 42–43; overview 40–41; pilot study 42; qualitative data collection 44–45; quantitative data collection 43–44; research tools 41–42
motivation see altruistic motivation; career-choice motivation scale (CCM Scale); intrinsic motivation; extrinsic motivation
motivational factors 18, 20, 24–25

Nanjing Nationalist Government 2
Nanyang Public School Teacher Education Institute 2
National College Entrance Examination (NCEE) scores 42
National Education Association national surveys 23
national teacher-training schools 2
New Education System 2
New Zealand pre-service teachers, career motivation 18
non-education programs 5
nonmetric variables 48
nonsignificant interaction effect 60

oblique rotations 53
Olaseboye Olasehinde, M. 19
one-year rural school service 88
online audio interviews 44–45, 66, 94
orthogonal rotations 53
overarching research questions see research questions/sub-questions
over-justification effect see undermining effect of extrinsic reward (UEER) theory

Papanastasiou, C. 20
Papanastasiou, E. 20
participants' contact information 43
participants, demographic information: family background 49; personal information 48–49; university profile 49–52
People's Republic of China (1949) 2, 41

People's Subsidies Scheme 2
personal interest in teaching *see* personal interest
personal interest: American pre-service teachers 22; comparison between self sponsored and policy funded teachers 58–59; definition 9, 55; funding status and gender relationships 59–60; funding status and year of study relationship 60–63; ignored 30; qualitative findings 63–64; quantitative analysis 55–56, 55
PFPTs narrative stories, ten cases: high-satisfaction group 66–73; low-satisfaction group 78–83; medium-satisfaction group 73–78; participants, demographic information of 66, 67; reflections 83–86
PFPTs and SSPTs: career-choice motivation, comparison of 58; independent-samples t-test results 59
policy-funded pre-service teachers (PFPTs): career choice motivation of 30–31; definition of 9; demographic information 48–52; quantitative research questions 12; *see also* PFPTs narrative stories, ten cases
pre-service teachers: American 22; Dutch 19, 28; Hong Kong SAR 21; Irish 19, 26; Jamaican 20; Macau SAR 21; New Zealand 18; Singaporean 19; Turkish (English) 20; UK pre-service teachers 22–23; *see also* Central Government-Funded Teacher Education (CGFTE) policy; Chinese pre-service teachers
principal component analysis (PCA) 52; results 53–58
professional postgraduate study opportunity 12, 88, 90; *see also* CGFTE encouraging terms
Provincial Executive Department of Education 5, 6

qualitative research question 13
quantitative data analysis: demographic information 48–52; exploratory factor analysis for CCM scale 52–58; impacts 58–63; independent-samples t test 58–63; missing data 47–48; research questions 52, 58; results 53–62; statistical techniques 52, 58; summary 63–64; two-way between-groups ANOVA 58–63
quantitative design 40–41
quantitative research questions 12–13
qualitative study methods 94

research discussion: conclusion 95–96; limitations and future studies 94–95; main findings 87–89; recommendations 89–94
research design *see* mixed-methods research design
research questions/sub-questions 12–13
Reform and Open-Door Policy (1978) 21
restrictive terms *see* CGFTE policy restrictive terms
Richardson, P. W. 18
rotated factor matrix 53
Rothland, M. 19
Rui Hao's story 66, 67, 77–78; *see also* PFPTs narrative stories, ten cases
rural schools/rural-area schools 3–7, 91, 92

"school-linked pursuits" (attractor) 24
school management jobs, availability of 12, 88; *see also* CGFTE policy encouraging terms
self-funded teacher education 3
self-sponsored pre-service teachers (SSPTs) 12, 48
semi-structured interview outline 41–42
service attractors 24
Sichuan Province 43
Sinclair, C. 18
Singaporean pre-service teachers, career motivation 19
"six-year teaching service" 88; *see also* CGFTE policy encouraging terms
Su, Z.-X. 22
"subjective warrant" (facilitator) 24
SurveyMonkey software 42

"task-specific value" 10, 11, 88, 95; *see also* Expectancy–Value Theory (EVT)
Teacher Education Act 2

teacher educators 6, 9, 20, 31, 92, 94
teacher influence 55, 57, 83, 96
teachers' career-choice motivations: attractors/facilitators 23–26; choice of teaching, factors influencing 26–29; different contexts 17–23
teacher-training programs 3, 4; CGFTE policy 5–7; government funded 8, 12; Indonesia 20; female pre-service teachers in 26; motivation to enter 30; reform 92–93
teacher-training school regulations 2
teacher–training universities: University A 43; University B 43; University C 43
tertiary education opportunities 3
theoretical foundations: expectancy–value theory (EVT) model 9–11; undermining effect of extrinsic reward (UEER) theory 11–12
three-dimensional model 31
tuition-free teacher education in China, history of 1–2
Turkish (English) pre-service teachers, career motivation 20

undermining effect of extrinsic reward (UEER) theory 11–12, 87, 89–90
UK pre-service teachers 22–23

univariate tests 59
urban-area schools 4
"utility value" 10; see also Expectancy–Value Theory (EVT)

varimax rotations, see orthogonal rotations
volitional behaviour identity (three-dimensional model) 31

Watt, H. M. G. 18
Weiner, B 9, 10
Wen Jiabao 4
Wen Jing's story 77; see also PFPTs narrative stories, ten cases
"wide decision range" (facilitator) 24

Xiao Fang's story 66, 67, 71–72; see also PFPTs narrative stories, ten cases

Yong, B. C. S. 20

Zhen Zhen's story 66, 67, 73–76; see also PFPTs narrative stories, ten cases
Zhao, H. 21
Zhu Min's story 66, 67, 80–82; see also PFPTs narrative stories, ten cases
Zimbabwe pre-service teachers, career motivation 19

For Product Safety Concerns and Information please contact our EU
representative GPSR@taylorandfrancis.com
Taylor & Francis Verlag GmbH, Kaufingerstraße 24, 80331 München, Germany

www.ingramcontent.com/pod-product-compliance
Lightning Source LLC
Chambersburg PA
CBHW071512150426
43191CB00009B/1498

Another superb publication from Adam Poole, whose original and thought-provoking work I have been following for some years now. With this new book, Poole urges us to look at the 'realities' of host country national teachers in a different light, questioning dominating concepts and voices in education research while privileging 'bricolage' from both China and the 'West'. Poole's book is a great example of decoloniality that will stimulate further critical research on teacherhood in international schools.

Professor Fred Dervin, *Professor of multicultural education, Faculty of Educational Sciences, University of Helsinki*

This is a timely and significant contribution to the international school literature. Host country national teachers are a growing presence in international schools in China, but to date they have received little scholarly attention. This book sheds light on the motivations of these teachers in a refreshing and engaging manner. It will be of interest to postgraduate students coming to the field of international schooling for the first time, as well as more experienced scholars wishing to update their knowledge about international schooling in China.

Dr Qin Yunyun, *Assistant Professor, The Graduate School of Education, Beijing Foreign Studies University*

This book offers an in-depth and constructive insight into the nature of the complex international schooling scene in China. Readers will find the book to be a useful reference to understanding the growth of international schools in China, and the type of educator that is getting involved. Moreover, the focus on host-nation teachers is both original and important. Overall, this is a compelling read, offering fresh perspectives and insights.

Dr Tristan Bunnell, *Senior Lecturer, University of Bath*